The ROYAL PALACES of SPAIN

The ROYAL PALACES of
SPAIN

Text by
JUAN A. HERNÁNDEZ FERRERO

Photographs by
HUMBERTO RIVAS

ABBEVILLE PRESS PUBLISHERS   NEW YORK   PARIS   LONDON

JACKET FRONT: *Main facade of La Granja de San Ildefonso, looking across the gardens* (see also pages 310–11).
JACKET BACK: *View of the Print Gallery in the Royal Library of El Escorial* (see also page 227).
ENDPAPERS: *Christ the Savior. Stucco medallion by Luis Salvador Carmona in the sacristy of Collegiate Church, La Granja de San Ildefonso* (see also pages 312–13).
FRONTISPIECE: *View of the Royal Chapel in the palace of Madrid* (see also page 147).
PAGES 4–5: *Vault fresco by Giovanni Battista Tiepolo in the Throne Room of the palace of Madrid* (see also pages 122–23).

ENGLISH-LANGUAGE EDITION
EDITOR: Jeanne D'Andrea
JACKET AND INTERIOR TYPOGRAPHIC DESIGN: Molly Shields
PRODUCTION EDITOR: Meredith Wolf Schizer
PRODUCTION MANAGER: Louis J. Bilka, Jr.

First edition
10 9 8 7 6 5 4 3 2 1

LIBRARY OF CONGRESS CATALOGING-IN-PUBLICATION DATA
Hernández Ferrero, Juan A.
    [Palacios reales del Patrimonio Nacional. English]
    The royal palaces of Spain / text by Juan A. Hernández Ferrero, photographs by Humberto Rivas.
        p.   cm.
    ISBN 0-7892-0501-7
    1. Palaces—Spain.   2. Spain—Kings and rulers—Dwellings.
I. Title.
NA7775.H4713 1998
728.8'2'0946—dc21   98-28566

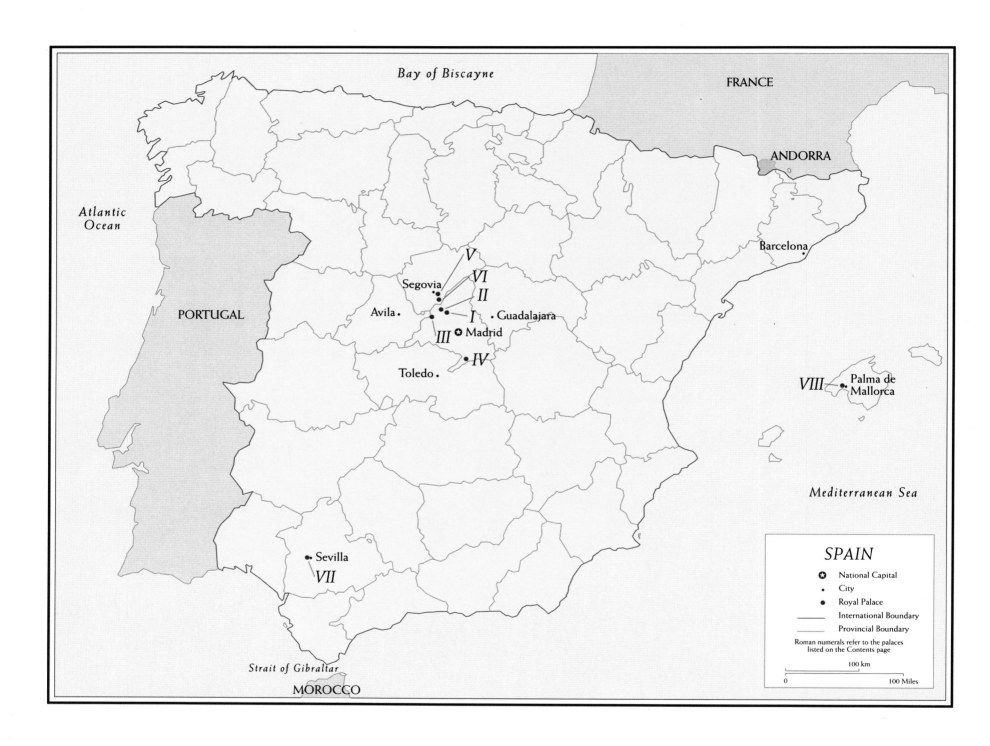

Bay of Biscayne

FRANCE

ANDORRA

Atlantic
Ocean

PORTUGAL

Barcelona

V

VI

Segovia

II

Avila

I

Guadalajara

III

Madrid

IV

Toledo

VIII

Palma de
Mallorca

Mediterranean Sea

Sevilla

VII

Strait of Gibraltar

MOROCCO

SPAIN

National Capital

City

Royal Palace

International Boundary

Provincial Boundary

Roman numerals refer to the palaces
listed on the Contents page

100 km

0   100 Miles

CONTENTS

PROLOGUE

✠

Beyond style, architecture has to be understood as a true source of memory, which explains the respect it inspires in all who experience it. Architecture gathers into its essence and appearance, its structure and ornament, all the events that take place at a given moment in history, conveying to us the spirit of a time. A knowledge of architecture is a way of approaching the past, using it as a guide, a sure witness to what once occurred.

Thus the aqueduct of Segovia tells us more about its Roman essence than all the scholarly treatises written about it. Wandering through the naves and chapels of Burgos Cathedral, or delighting in the Nazarite palaces of La Alhambra, one clearly feels something undefinable, which is simply the evocative power of architecture. Such power permeates and delights our senses and for a few instants makes us abandon the real time in which we live. There is no need to fantasize about other eras. Architecture is a virtual time machine.

Architecture speaks to the scholar and the layman alike, in a way both are able to understand. If, in addition, a knowledgeable architectural emissary takes us on a stroll like this one through the royal palaces of the Spanish Crown, then the pleasure is complete. Indeed, Juan Hernández Ferrero has two very important qualifications: his profession as an architect and his interest in history. He has written an admirable text based on his intimate knowledge of these palace complexes. As curator architect of the National Heritage, he oversees, maintains, restores, and preserves these buildings. Those of us who are privileged to be his friends know that he performs this highly demanding task not only as a duty but with love. In his writing architecture and historic circumstances tend to explain each other.

The excellent pictorial accompaniment in this book is in itself a treat for the eye. It intensifies the memory and transmits the inexpressible beauty of these royal buildings. A rich chapter on courtly art was written in these palaces, particularly during the sixteenth and seventeenth centuries, not to mention the artists of the Baroque period, such as Velázquez, who worked for the Hapsburg king Felipe IV in the now vanished Alcázar of Madrid and whose masterpieces were later moved to the Prado Museum.

From their medieval prologue in Mallorca and Sevilla, these palace buildings, fountains, and gardens project a European cosmopolitanism befitting the court. Their language is universal and can be heard in other European capitals as well, where the external signs of taste, refinement, power, and wealth stimulated and promoted rivalry, above all in the eighteenth century. Absolute rulers contended for the services of prestigious architects and painters such as Juvarra, Mengs, and Tiepolo in order to produce better buildings or frescoes than their predecessors or contemporaries. They competed to emulate rooms paneled in mirrors, porcelain, or fine woods; to produce superior objects of bronze, glass, and pietre dure; to own fountains in the manner of Versailles. These were the enticements that spurred a line of art history that parallels the distinctive artistic evolution of each country. The fashions of France and Italy were reflected in Madrid and St. Petersburg. And from France and Italy artists and craftsmen arrived in Spain to build the Royal Palace of Madrid or the fountains and gardens of La Granja, shining pages of European art grafted on the Spanish horizon under the rule of the Hapsburg and Bourbon kings.

PEDRO NAVASCUÉS PALACIOS

INTRODUCTION

✠

A large and varied exhibition of the Vatican collections opened at New York's Metropolitan Museum of Art in February 1983. After four months in New York, the show traveled to the Art Institute of Chicago and then to the Fine Arts Museum in San Francisco for three-month periods.

This exhibition was the largest effort ever made by a foreign institution to show its masterpieces in the United States, and it presented a vast and carefully chosen selection of the riches stored in the Vatican Museums to the American public.

Objects as highly esteemed as the *Apollo Belvedere*, the *Belvedere Torso*, the *Athena and Marsyas* group, Bernini's *Bust of Urban VIII*, the *Good Shepherd* marble, the *Burial of Christ* by Caravaggio, *Saint Jerome* by Leonardo da Vinci, several altarpieces by Raphael, and the Van Aelst tapestry *The Miracle of the Fishes* after a Raphael design were accompanied by dozens of other superb pieces. The exhibition included marbles and mosaics, fabrics and portrait busts, tapestries and bronzes, dalmatics, chalices and medallions, panel paintings and canvases, an assemblage capable of stirring the most disinterested observer. Almost two hundred pieces spanned two thousand years of history, from works of Republican Rome to a Henri Matisse collage. For many, the *opera prima* was the extraordinarily well-preserved marble statue, the *Augustus Prima Porta.*

The show was authorized by Pope John Paul II in 1982 from the Vatican to gratefully acknowledge his previous visit to the United States. In his remarks the Pope spoke of the millennia-old relationship between the papacy and the arts, of the ability of man to attain the beauty that captivates him, and of a renewal by this generation of the Church's interest in art and culture.

The marvelous objects on exhibition made a deep impression on viewers, and many European visitors questioned why they needed to cross the Atlantic to see an assemblage of art that many of them could reach in a day's journey by car, or in an eighty- or ninety-minute flight from their own countries. The simple answer is that modern culture operates through carefully planned events that stimulate public interest. The ritual of anniversaries and centennials and large exhibitions, is capable of renewing areas and cities, of awakening the spirit, and of reminding us of our origins.

Strolling along Fifth Avenue back to their hotels visitors also asked themselves what other European institutions, what other nobles and princes, what other palaces or museums could offer the Metropolitan such a rich and diverse exhibition as this one. There were varied, even original answers, but they all shared one criterion. Only institutions with long histories could accumulate such riches: centuries-old monarchies like the English, cultural hubs and crucibles like Paris or Venice, general museums like the British Museum or the Louvre, or famous palaces with the grand historic-artistic breath of Versailles, Fontainebleau, Barberini, Pitti, or Saint James.

The answers to these questions would have been more precise if one were to focus on the most brilliant eras that these collections represent: Renaissance and Baroque. These seem to be the most interesting moments, because of the creative explosion of those periods and the general appreciation of ancient art that was brought up to date by Renaissance and Baroque styles. And Renaissance monarchs were as busy commissioning paintings and statues from artists of their own time as they were pressing their numerous agents for more ancient and medieval art and artifacts for their private collections.

Louis XIV, Richelieu, Charles V, Lorenzo de Medici, not to mention Julius II, Urban VII and other popes, were among the many great patrons of the time. The geographic centers of this phenomenon were Paris, London, Rome, and Venice.

Palaces were the frames and stages for the life and feats of the great Renaissance and Baroque nobles, and palace architecture acquired great significance as these buildings became vigorous symbols of political and social power. The Renaissance and Baroque palace was the home of the noble, prince, or king, the physical place where he and his family were born, baptized, educated, and married, where he wielded power and where he finally died. The palace is not only the personal residence of the ruler but also the institutional seat of his power. Thus a relationship is created among the material, ideal, conceptual, and functional elements of the architecture, which interpenetrate, each at the service of the others. This interpretation makes it impossible to read and interpret a Baroque palace without evoking its condition as a historic-artistic center of power and without considering the lives of its residents.

Palace architecture as the "face of power" is an idea that occurs at least as early as the Middle Ages, if not before. The feudal castle is certainly the clearest portrayal of the lord's power and the physical symbol of vassalage. But Renaissance and Baroque palaces, although they possess these characteristics, are much richer and more complex. They are symbols of power but also of the monarch's munificence and generosity. In addition to exercising power, he is trained in and sensitive to the arts, which gives him a high degree of spiritual satisfaction as well as the admiration that such qualities elicit among his subjects.

It has often been said that Renaissance and Baroque palaces are especially appropriate for analyzing these phenomena and deepening our knowledge and understanding of the sixteenth, seventeenth, and eighteenth centuries. This assertion is true but incomplete. Indeed, the study of the palaces of these centuries is highly useful for an understanding of the political, social, and cultural life of those years. This, however, is because there is abundant pictorial and written information from that period, while information on medieval residences is lacking. Original medieval architectural plans are scarce, while they become numerous from the time of the Renaissance. The abundant

research data the modern age offers, compared with the middle and ancient periods, makes the Renaissance and Baroque palaces a more attractive and reliable subject for historical study than feudal buildings or the architecture of the Visigothic or Roman empires. These reflections, in the wake of the Vatican exhibition, take us readily to Venice, Michelangelo, Leonardo, Borromini, Henry VIII, or Louis XIV, and to palaces like La Farnesina, Chambord, or Windsor.

Here, a striking fact comes to mind: the palaces of the Spanish Crown built from 1500 to 1800 were totally unknown to most visitors to New York's exhibition at the Metropolitan. Yet these buildings house a wealth of tapestries, paintings, architectural details, sculpture, and decorative arts of such quality and number that they may well constitute the only Western European collections that can measure up to those of the Vatican.

Palaces such as El Escorial, El Pardo, or La Granja were as well furnished as the best palaces of their times in neighboring countries. And the Spanish kings Felipe II, Felipe IV, and Carlos III were as knowledgeable about the arts and culture as the most specialized and sensitive of their contemporaries.

The Spanish kings, from the fifteenth and sixteenth centuries to the present, have devoted large sums of money and human resources toward increasing their cultural legacy and preserving their ancestral heritage. From the late fifteenth century some twenty Spanish sovereigns, with few exceptions, were unceasing in their personal and institutional efforts to create and preserve an extraordinary group of collections. Fortunately, the nucleus of these collections has withstood the advance of time, the winds of war, and the adverse turns of history as well as the political and administrative whims of many epochs. With their five-hundred-year history, many of the palaces and gardens, fountains and statues, paintings and tapestries as well as other exceptional objects have not lasted or are no longer intact. Nonetheless, what is left provides a very good idea of what has been the continuing will of the Spanish monarchy in the cultural arena. The royal collections and magnificent palaces have grown from this determination to become amazing depositories of art.

To better understand this process of collecting under the aegis of the Spanish Crown and to study the growth and development of these collections, one has to turn back half a millennium to the late Middle Ages in Spain.

✛

On the morning of October 19, 1469, in the "salón rico" (rich hall) of the Vivero Palace, in the city of Valladolid, a young couple named Fernando and Isabel (Ferdinand and Isabella) were married. Fernando, then seventeen years old, was king of Sicily and heir to the crown of Aragón. Isabel, one year older, was heiress to the Castilian crown.

Their union had many powerful enemies, from Louis XI of France to a large part of the Castilian nobility, including King Enrique IV, brother of Isabel, and Pope Paul II who had promised but not granted the required papal dispensation. It was more than a wedding between a prince and a princess. The extraordinary political talent of the young Fernando, who shortly afterward revealed himself as one of the political geniuses of the Renaissance and the extremely fine intuition and tenacity of Isabel, were joined to build a very firm basis for three decades of deep political and strategic transformations that would have repercussions on three continents.

In only thirty years, Isabel and Fernando were able to unify the Iberian peninsula except for Portugal, which remained independent. The fall of the last Muslim stronghold in 1492—the coveted kingdom of Granada—and the incorporation of the kingdom of Navarra some years later are events that drafted a new geopolitical map of Spain that was inconceivable in the mid-fifteenth century. At the end of the century, the Spanish Crown had overcome the bitter medieval sense of a "lost Spain," brought on by the defeat of Visigothic Spain by the Muslim invasion in the early eighth century. A new Spain, with transformed institutions, was settling with force in the peninsula. The year 1492 was pivotal: in January the long struggle to reconquer the peninsula ended with the fall of Granada; in October Columbus's first expedition, financed by Queen Isabel, arrived on American land after sailing west for several months.

These were the best tidings for continuing to build a unification policy. Several kingdoms united under the same crown: Castilla and Aragón, Granada and Navarra, not to mention the marriage links with Portugal. Administrative unity and the reinforcement of royal power

came with a notable loss of power by the nobility and the knighthood. Religious unity (hence, the reference to the royal couple as the Catholic Monarchs) explains the politics of events as momentous as the expulsion of the Jews, foreign policy in North Africa, and the creation of the Inquisition.

These are transformations so far-reaching that, aside from constituting a broad historical change, they signify something as novel as the creation of a new state, the modern state, solid and strong, far from the weak and blurred late medieval state. Indeed, the phrase "to be living in modern times" was already being heard.

A necessary requirement of the new state was to bring about the creation of a stable court, in a fixed place, as opposed to the itinerant courts of the Castilian and Aragonese monarchs before Fernando and Isabel. But settling the Spanish court in a permanent place, a capital city of Spain, was left to future generations. Fernando and Isabel, for historical, political, and military reasons, lived in many peninsular locations, in a sense carrying the court on their backs. Medina del Campo, Ubeda, Burgos, Sos, Madrigal, Sevilla, Barcelona, Valencia, Santa Fe, Granada, are just some of the places where the sovereigns stayed in the last third of the fifteenth century.

Nevertheless, a permanently settled court and a capital city were already being heralded. Their creation, however, was reserved for the grandson of the royal couple, a Burgundian born in Ghent in 1500, whose name was Carlos (Carlos I, King of Spain; later the Holy Roman Emperor Charles V).

This dream of a capital and a stable court was accompanied by extraordinary and meaningful events. Understandably, the energies of the Crown were directed mainly to political and military objectives, but these rulers were also engaged in art patronage. In 1492, the year renowned for so many remarkable events, the first chamber painter of the Spanish court was appointed. Michel Sittow came from Estonia, and he was known in Spain as Melchor Alemán. (Melchor was derived from Michel; *alemán*, meaning German, was the surname given to anyone from beyond the Rhine or the Elbe.)

At the same time as Sittow, another artist was working in Spain, Juan de Flandes, who was also a northerner. The tradition of painting, architecture, and sculpture in those areas was impressive. Gil de Siloé,

Juan Guas, Enrique Egás, Hannequin of Brussels, and Jochen of Utrecht are just a few of the most popular artists of the time. The list of artists at the service of the Spanish court had to begin with these men brought from the north.

Very few visitors today notice that Sittow's *Portrait of an Unknown Man* in the Mauritshuis of The Hague is an austere Castilian face. And few remember that the *Lives of Christ and the Virgin* in the collection of the National Heritage (the body in charge of the Spanish royal collections) is one of the masterpieces of Juan de Flandes. The painting is shown today in the Royal Palace of Madrid. The other great picture by the same painter is a delightful portrait of Queen Isabel, his patroness and protector, and it hangs in the main hall of the Palace of El Pardo, a few kilometers from Madrid. Only a few specialists recall that General Franco worked in his office there for thirty-five years beside this portrait of the Catholic Queen Isabel.

The establishment of a settled modern state was the work of the grandson of Fernando and Isabel, Carlos I (Carlos V, or Charles V, Holy Roman Emperor from 1519–1556). History shows that despite his efforts to pursue a stable court or a Spanish capital—Toledo was his choice—events took another direction. A final location for the Spanish capital with its constellation of palaces had to wait for the next generation, that of his son Felipe II.

The many government seats, royal houses, military camps, and settlements of Isabel and Fernando, were passed on to Carlos I. Carlos traveled constantly, not by choice but because his imperial duties made it inevitable. He would like to have created a stable court and a settled state, but the difficult circumstances of his time prevented this. He traveled incessantly from the time he was seventeen. In 1517 he left Flanders for Spain, where he stayed for thirty-two months. He then went to Germany and England, returning to Spain by mid-1522 for seven years. In 1529 he traveled to Bologna to receive one of the imperial crowns, and then somewhat later went to Innsbruck, Munich, and other central European cities. In 1532 he went to Vienna, moving on to Italy, and then back to Spain in April 1533. After this stay in Spain, where he lived for two years in the Alcázar of Madrid and readied an expedition to Tunisia and Sicily, he made trips to Naples and Rome. In Spain again in December 1536, he left in

spring 1538, to return three months later and remain for fourteen months. By the end of 1539, his wife Isabel now dead, Carlos went to France, led a punitive action against Ghent, the city of his birth, and came back to Spain, making a long, roundabout trip through Italy.

The emperor arrived in Spain in November 1541 for another stay, next to the last, this time for eighteen months. In May 1543 he left Spain again and remained away for thirteen years, spending time in Spira, Regensburg, Halle, Augsburg, Innsbruck, Metz, and many other cities. In 1555, in Brussels, he abdicated; and the following year he returned to Spain, for the last time. He died there two years later in Yuste.

Was any more activity in forty years of public life possible for a sovereign in the first half of the sixteenth century? Was a higher concentration of political, religious, and military problems possible in a relatively short life? Few men in his time endured more political and human tensions than Carlos I.

Not surprisingly, the task of building a modern state and its architectural environment fell to Carlos's son, Felipe II. Nevertheless, Carlos I showed his imperial drive in the construction of a palace in Granada and in various modifications of the alcazars of Toledo and Madrid. But because these buildings are not royal palaces today, they are beyond the scope of this book.

El Pardo is the most important contribution of Carlos I to the buildings with royal palace status today. Although it was begun by him, other circumstances prevented him from following its construction with the tenacity and sustained attention of some of his successors. He was also involved in the very earliest stage of Aranjuez. And although he did not have the time to develop architectural and city-planning projects in and around the imperial capital of Toledo, El Pardo and Aranjuez were good beginnings. Finished examples of his desire to be active in this arena are Granada and the Reales Alcázares in Sevilla.

Felipe II (1527–1598) inherited his father's major problems— the French, the Turks, and the Protestant uprising. Thus Felipe's foreign policy was practically the same as his father's. The young prince was a traveler, too, but not to the same extent as Carlos I. England, Italy, Austria, Flanders, France, were the stages of his early activity.

But what contributed most to the difference between their foreign policies, and also released Felipe from the pressure to travel, was his freedom from imperial obligations. When Carlos appointed his brother Fernando to succeed him as emperor, Felipe's hope of ruling the empire was lost.

Fernando, three years younger than Carlos, was born in Alcalá de Henares. A full Spaniard by birth, language, education, and mind-set, he was destined to successfully carry out a European policy based on religious tolerance. Fernando I of Bohemia, the name history has given him, participated actively in the Augsburg Peace of 1555, and he was elected emperor in 1558, an office he discharged until his death in Vienna six years later. Fernando, who inherited the political abilities of his grandfather and namesake, Fernando the Catholic, urgently deserves a well-balanced biography.

Juana la Loca, mother of Carlos and Fernando, would never have imagined that Carlos, born in Ghent and fully dedicated to Europe, would become increasingly more Spanish and decide to retire and die in a remote corner of Extremadura. Nor could she imagine that her other son, Fernando, the most Spanish of her children, was to play such a decisive role in the government of his domains in central Europe. Juana died in 1555 without knowing that her second son also took the imperial crown.

Felipe II returned to Castilla from Flanders in autumn 1559, when he was thirty-two years old, and he remained in the Iberian Peninsula for the rest of his life (later becoming king of Portugal as well). He was now King Don Felipe of Spain, his Catholic Majesty, twice widowed, intelligent, scheming, with an artistic taste formed in England, France, Flanders, and Italy. His knowledge of mathematics, architecture, and the humanities was considerable. Imperial duties had passed to the line of his uncle and Viennese cousins. The freedom this gave Felipe as well as his dedication to peninsular affairs from 1559 had important repercussions on the construction of Spanish palaces.

On his return to Spain, Felipe II made two striking decisions only eighteen months apart. The first was the appointment on July 15, 1559, of Juan Bautista de Toledo as royal architect. This appointment anticipated the idea of El Escorial—the idea of a great commemorative monastery, the crystallization of Felipe's complex personality that was taking firm shape in the royal mind. A little less than four years after this appointment, the cornerstone of the colossus of El Escorial was laid. Felipe's second key decision was to move the capital of Carlos I from the imperial city of Toledo to the modest city of Madrid, where there was only an old alcazar and a few minor churches surrounded by a motley of unattractive houses.

This move had major political meaning for a number of reasons. One was that it represented a radical change in thinking about the location of the capital. Carlos had opted for Toledo because, in addition to his liking for the city, he saw in it a capital-city culture with a depth that came from Roman and Visigothic times, not to mention eight medieval centuries. Toledo was the Roman Toletum, the seat of the Visigothic bishops' councils and the main city reconquered in the time of El Cid by Alfonso VI of Castilla (1030–1109). The figure of Alfonso and the ideals of his age are exemplified by his advance to the Tagus line and the fall of Toledo in 1085. Toledo was also the Catholic Primate's see, and a grand Gothic urban center developed around its cathedral in the fourteenth and fifteenth centuries. In short, the inclination of Carlos I to favor Toledo was as logical as the decision of Felipe II to deprive Toledo of her status as capital seems illogical. This is especially so since the city favored by the royal decision was a rather insignificant hamlet around an old alcazar.

Why did Felipe II prefer Madrid? There may be more than one reason, but each is very complex. A purely geographic factor may have influenced the king's will: Madrid is located in the center of the peninsula and Felipe II admired, indeed venerated, the radial system. This concern with geometry is not a trifling one, although it may seem to us far removed from politics, because geometry in the sixteenth century had more varied and arcane meanings. The model of a basic geometric plan was undoubtedly on the minds of the king and his advisers. It would be a static solar system, with a court center in Madrid's Alcázar, surrounded by residential areas relatively nearby. El Pardo and incipient Aranjuez were a half day's journey away and the Casa del Bosque in Balsaín one day's journey. The basic scheme of the initial design was to be a court with satellites: the main household in Madrid's Alcázar, a house for hunting in El Pardo, a house by the river in Aranjuez, and a house in the forest (Casa del Bosque) on the other side of the mountains, in Segovian lands, on the road to Valladolid. One official center, the Alcázar in Madrid, and three peripheral homes, Balsaín, Aranjuez, and El Pardo, surrounded by woods and game, were very much to the royal taste.

Where did this simple arrangement come from? or better, where had Felipe seen something similar? Probably in the princely residences he visited in the north of Italy, or even in Flanders with its centrally located Brussels. But the likeliest model may be the London Tower, with its constellation of small palaces, castles, and defensive redoubts, arranged in a circular plan of clear and precise geometry. During his more than two years in London, Felipe had had the chance to observe and study this solution.

☩

Thus the historic starting point for the array of Spanish royal palaces was, on one hand, the will to create a proper court at a fixed point, instead of the itinerant mobility of medieval times. The unexpected choice of Madrid satisfied the new monarchy's need for a political and geometric center that would enable the *new state* to "live in modern times." On the other hand, political, physical, and economic opportunities were needed in order to establish and materialize this court. The task of creating a Spanish court now fell to Felipe II in the second half of the sixteenth century.

This historical moment imposed new artistic and political considerations as well as symbolic ones. The palace of the *princeps* had always been a symbol of power, apart from being the monarch's residence. Thus, the palace was linking its strong symbolic meaning with its new meaning as a house. For the Renaissance, it also became the materialization of an entire doctrine, of an assemblage of ideas made into building stones, canvases, sculptures, and gardens. The palace undoubtedly would be a facade of power and domination, but imbued with a very complex expressivity that displayed the desires, accomplishments, and aspirations of its owner. This includes his frustrations as well. This maze of ideas, expressed through the arts and in building projects, is as visible in newly erected palaces and buildings as it is in those that were rebuilt, enlarged, or modified. But these ideas and acts of will, displays and desires, artistic and sociopolitical epiphanies, do

not begin and end with the physical limitations of palace architecture. Even the more introverted buildings, forced by topography or the monarch's will to turn in on themselves, are systems that influence their landscape and environment in such a way that a purely architectural analysis is always incomplete. And if this occurs on an individual scale, it is even truer when these systems are viewed as a whole. Since the central court and its satellite palaces are a collection of systems, analysis requires us to look at each one individually as well as with a combined vision. This vision is indispensable for penetrating, however superficially, their more transcendent meaning. Thus the study of these royal buildings, their origins, architecture, and decor, their names and locations, the historic memories retained within their walls and surroundings, yields a rather accurate reconstruction of the attitudes and spirit of the past.

The Spanish royal palaces of the period from 1500 to 1800 that still exist on this threshold of the twenty-first century are ideal for this historic analysis, because they possess unique and highly interesting features.

☩

Observed from afar, two high points stand out from the medieval Spanish landscape, breaking its horizontality: churches and castles. They are two symbols of power: the religious power of the Church, represented by belfries and spires; and the political power of the nobility, manifested in castles and towers.

The evolution of this mentality began about 1500, and these two powers, represented by these very visible architectural elements, changed substantially with the loss of socio-military ground by the aristocracy. The castle, that outstanding sign of feudal lordship, ceased to have meaning as the command of armies passed on to the king.

But monarchy by Divine Right was strongly rooted and enjoyed a general acceptance in Spain. And thus, from that time, the king's household, the palace, symbolizes the union of both political and religious powers. Not as in Britain, where the monarch was, and still is after half a millennium, the head of the Anglican Church. Rather it was based on the certainty that the power of Carlos I, Felipe II, and their successors was granted by God, coming directly from God in a kind of sublime transmission accepted by the entire society. This idea provided the Spanish royal palaces with a unique architectural configuration. The church, chapel, or basilica, become key elements in the plans for new construction, or else highly singular elements added to earlier buildings.

Fernando Chueca Goitia, the noted architect and architectural historian, explained this concept with admirable clarity and precision in his *Royal Houses in Spanish Monasteries and Convents*, published more than thirty years ago. This union of religious and civil powers existed in the convents and monasteries of the late Spanish Middle Ages, and it is not surprising that Spanish royal palaces from that time until the twentieth century can be keenly analyzed in this light. The architectural layouts, plans, elevations, and cross-sections of the palaces clearly show their dual nature.

Just as most Spanish royal palaces cannot be understood through only an intramural study, surrounded as they are by parks and gardens, esplanades, plazas, and loggias, one cannot forget the visual transcendence of the religious element. The church has a functional, liturgical, and symbolic mission that does not turn inward but transcends the stone boundaries of its architecture. The most striking case of this is that of the rosaries outside the hermitages around the Spanish royal houses. This is very clear in the case of Madrid's Buen Retiro palace, which has now disappeared. Aranjuez also had this network of hermitages in the seventeenth century, which King Felipe IV no doubt saw in Montserrat and then built in his palace. The role played by the church or chapel in the context of the palace deserves special attention. Without this awareness El Escorial, Aranjuez, Madrid, and Riofrío cannot be understood.

Spanish royal palaces can also be studied through analyses made from the viewpoints of topography and place names. These seemingly secondary matters provide insights to an understanding of the origin of these royal buildings and the decisions that made them a reality.

Another fundamental factor that knits together all of these historic buildings was the kings' munificence. Viewed by the monarchs as generosity, it was actually used as a propaganda tool that allowed them to mobilize enormous financial and human resources. This, in turn, strengthened the rulers in the eyes of their subjects and exalted their image for posterity. Renaissance and Baroque rulers found it much more appealing to be remembered for a grand palace surrounded by gardens than for a piece of literature or an excellent musical score composed by the prince himself.

The royal palaces of the Spanish Crown discussed in this book can be divided into three groups. First, La Almudaina Royal Palace in Palma de Majorca and the Reales Alcázares in Seville. Both are today official residences of the Spanish sovereigns in those cities and deserve to be mentioned first, since they are the oldest Spanish royal houses that retain that status. Each has a different background, cultural origin, and development; but they have some common features, such as names and locations. *Almudaina* in Arabic means "citadel," or "walled and fortified enclosure within a city." *Alcázar*, from Arabic *al-ksar*, "the palace," derives in turn from Latin *castrum*, "a fortified town" or "an army encampment."

The relative locations of these fortresses are similar. From the time of its Roman origin the Almudaina in Palma has been on a point dominating the arch of the bay, and its east facade naturally faces the shore, while the north facade once faced the *riera* (river). The riverbed is now the Borne promenade, since the river was deflected in the seventeenth century into a channel to the west.

The old Arab alcazar in Sevilla was on the banks of the Guadalquivir. In earlier times this river flowed approximately where the Avenida de la Constitución now runs, with the Gothic cathedral on one side. More than a thousand years ago the Muslim alcazar was also by a river.

Very few royal palaces, not only in Europe but throughout the world, are two millennia old and still function as royal residences. In 1984 the central section of La Almudaina was renovated to house the Spanish monarchs and their guests; and in 1991 the wing of the Sevillian Reales Alcázares that surrounds the courtyard of Doña María de Padilla was renovated to lodge the royal family.

The second group of Spanish royal palaces—still in use as palaces and also as museums open to the public—is comprised of El Pardo, Aranjuez, and El Escorial. These three palaces were begun in the sixteenth century, although this has to be qualified. El Pardo was a hunting ground for the Trastámara dynasty in the late Middle Ages, and it is located in a large, hilly holm-oak forest on the southern skirts of the Guadarrama range. The name *Pardo* (brown) comes from this large patch of brownish holm oaks. The first palace or royal house on this site was built in the mid-sixteenth century by Carlos I. The stone decoration of what was the main entrance on its west front, now a secondary entrance, is inscribed with the date 1548. El Pardo is a royal palace surrounded by a hunting forest.

Aranjuez, beside the Tagus River, also has a hunting origin, and it too was begun by Carlos I. Part of the land was expropriated and another part purchased from the Order of the Knights of Santiago by Carlos's grandparents, Fernando and Isabel. It seems that there was once a house for the master of the Order in this area, and names of the towns near Aranjuez help to confirm the Order's dominion of this land. A glance at a modern map provides names such as Uclés, Horcajo de Santiago, Villarrubia de Santiago, and Quintanar de la Orden.

If El Pardo palace cannot be understood without the 15,000 hectares of brown holm-oak forest that envelop it, Aranjuez cannot be separated from its marvelous gardens on the banks of the Tagus. Most of the splendor of this riverside park originated in the eighteenth century, although much of its design comes from the sixteenth. Thus El Pardo and Aranjuez are royal sites that Carlos I began to develop, projects that were completed, or at least continued, by his son Felipe II.

The third grand royal palace of this sixteenth-century group is El Escorial. Felipe's colossal monument was begun in 1563, when the king was thirty-six years old, and it was officially completed in 1584, with finishing and decoration work several years later. Recent linguistic research does not attribute the use of the term *escorial* (slag heap) to the probable deposit of residues from the foundries that might have been in the area but rather to the Latin *quercus*, the botanical name for the genus oak. Adding the prefix *es-*, it became *esquercus* and then evolved to *escorial*.

El Escorial is on a gentle slope of Mount Abantos in the Casarrubio district, a part of Segovia, in the sixteenth century when Segovian land covered a larger area than the present province. Felipe II purchased an immense tract of land encompassing several municipalities—accurately traceable today—to serve a great monastic foundation. The name monastery masks its true identity somewhat because, although it is known as the Monasterio de El Escorial, it was much more. It housed a college, a seminary, a hospital, a large library, a formidable basilica, and a royal residence. It was Felipe II's palace.

Felipe's Casa del Bosque deserves a brief comment here. It was the king's house in the Balsaín forest in Segovia. Only a nostalgic memory remains of this palace, which is now no more than a ruin among the little houses of the village. Balsaín, like Aranjuez and El Pardo, also began as a place for hunting. By the mid-fourteenth century, Enrique III of Trastámara had a hunting house there, but the palace was the personal decision of Felipe II, who ordered its construction about 1552. The palace was arranged around a central courtyard, peculiarly, with the king's quarters oriented to the north and the queen's to the south, a scheme opposite that of Aranjuez and El Escorial. The building was completed with an exquisite private garden, several square towers, a yard called *de vacas* (of cows), and a Flemish flavor in its upper floor and pyramidal spires. The entire complex was connected by walls and loggias.

A splendid view of this palace painted by Juan Bautista del Mazo, Velázquez's son-in-law, is in El Escorial. Isabel Clara Eugenia, the beloved daughter of Felipe II, was born in Balsaín on August 12, 1566, and taken to the baptismal font by her stepbrother Carlos and her uncle Juan de Austria.

The third group of palaces belongs to the eighteenth century: the Royal Palace in Madrid, and the palaces of La Granja de San Ildefonso and Riofrío. These three are the product of the rather unexpected drive of Felipe V, Spain's first Bourbon king. In a way, they are glittering symbols of the new dynasty. It seems as if the new French-born king, arriving on Spanish soil, needed a potent symbolic and visual device to affirm his identity and legitimacy in the very court of Madrid and the surrounding area.

The Royal Palace in Madrid is a grandiose and costly work on which Felipe V and his wife, Isabel de Farnesio (Isabella Farnese) placed their dreams and large sums of money. Known as the New Palace during the first century of its life, it was built on the land occupied by the old Alcázar, which had been partially destroyed by fire in 1734. Fourteen years earlier, Felipe V had begun to build his own new royal site in the French Bourbon style. This was to be a grand palace-alcázar in San Ildefonso, near the ancient Casa del Bosque in Balsaín, surrounded by magnificent gardens and the greatest display of sculptural fountains Spain had ever seen. La Granja de San Ildefonso would have been the grand Spanish Bourbon palace, if the fire in Madrid's Alcázar had not offered the king the opportunity to build a great court palace in Madrid as the center around which the other satellite palaces revolved.

There is still another Bourbon palace, Riofrío, begun by Queen Isabel Farnese, the widow of Felipe V, in about 1751. This new royal palace is small and pretty, built to the image of its older brother in Madrid, within a royal game preserve crossed by the river that gives the palace its name, Riofrío (cold river). Although Riofrío is said to lack history, it has its own past, small and delicate, sad and nostalgic.

Carlos III substantially changed the decorative plan of the new palace and added a new wing to the east facade. And, with his architect Sabbatini, he doubled the size of El Pardo and enlarged the palace at Aranjuez with two wings to the west. Carlos IV altered the north wing of El Escorial and its decor; and Isabel II gave a new look to the southern environs of the palace in Madrid. But all of this is part of the almost inevitable natural growth of these complexes.

Another palace worth mentioning has now disappeared. This is the Buen Retiro. Built in the first half of the seventeenth century by the Count-Duke of Olivares as a gift to his king, Felipe IV, it was completed rather quickly and enhanced with superb paintings, but it lasted no more than a century and a half. The wind of history swept it from the face of Madrid.

In summary, the Spanish Crown possesses two millennial palaces, one in Palma de Mallorca and the other in Sevilla. Three more palaces laden with symbolic, artistic, and historic value date from the Renaissance and Baroque periods: El Pardo, Aranjuez, and El Escorial. These palaces coincide with the Hapsburg dynasty in Spain. And there are three palaces from the eighteenth century—La Granja, Madrid, and Riofrío—as a stylistic consequence of dynastic change and Bourbon centralism. All of these palaces are still in full use by the Spanish royal family.

✠

The PALACE of MADRID

✠

The PALACE of MADRID

✠

The history of Madrid's Royal Palace begins on Christmas Eve of 1734, the night the old Alcázar burned. While the royal family was at the Palace of El Pardo for the holidays, fire broke out in the Alcázar, affecting the central part of the building between the two courtyards and adjacent areas. Chronicles relate that not until early January was the fire extinguished and the valuable objects retrieved. Many paintings, chalices, jewels, and relics were lost or damaged. The fire was a heavy loss for the royal collections, and although a precise inventory of destroyed items is not available, the losses must have been significant.

The fire destroyed paintings by Velázquez and Rubens, the architectural drawings of Herrera and Gómez de Mora, and the large tapestries that covered the Alcázar walls. What was the chapel of the lost Alcázar like, or the room where Velázquez painted *Las Meninas*, or the bedrooms of Felipe IV and Carlos II? Where was the dungeon where Felipe II confined his son Carlos until his death? Where were the *covachuelas*, the little nooks where political matters were determined, or the Casa del Tesoro where bureaucrats issued the documents of the kingdom?

It was a terrible loss. Madrid has no surplus of centuries-old buildings, and had this one survived—no matter how decrepit, altered, or restored—it would now be the most eminent and beloved building in Madrid. Half of modern Spanish history had vanished.

A malevolent legend places a certain blame on Felipe V, or at least accuses him of negligence. But this is untrue. The new king was very respectful of the Spanish palaces he found when he acceded to the throne, which was won after a long and painful War of Succession (1701–1714) in Spain and abroad. Names such as Almansa, Brihuega,

and Villaviciosa, as well as Ramillies and Oudernade, are reminders of the bloody battles fought between the Franco-Spanish troops and the allies of the Austrian Empire who defended the rights of the archduke. Long years of tensions were eased when the archduke took over the imperial crown, opening the way to the Spanish throne for the Bourbon dynasty, which brought an era of peace to Spain.

About 1720 Felipe V selected a place near the Casa del Bosque in Balsaín, and ordered the construction of a new palace next to a nearby Hieronymite hermitage. It was to be surrounded by gardens and fountains, taking advantage of the northern slopes and the Guadarrama range. The palace, La Granja de San Ildefonso, would be his house and his tomb. This was manifest neglect of the pantheon of the Austrian dynasty, El Escorial, for which he felt no liking. But the Alcázar fire shattered the king's train of thought, and he made two crucial decisions: demolish what was left of the Alcázar and build the best palace in Europe on the same site to display the spirit and magnificence of the Bourbon dynasty.

With these decisions, Felipe V erased the oldest mark of the previous dynasty, but at the same time he respected the magic of the site to maintain him as the "heir with the best right" to the Spanish Crown. What was the place he respected and what would the New Palace be like? The place, a knoll over the Manzanares River, where a Moorish castle once stood (*"Madrid's famous castle/allays the Moorish king's fears,"* says an old ballad). The castle was a link in the chain of fortresses that formed the defensive arch of medieval Toledo. Christian armies descending from the mountains following the river valleys, particularly the Guadarrama and the Manzanares, would find those two routes closed by castles. Recent excavations in the Plaza de

Oriente facing the Madrid palace have uncovered at least one watchtower adjacent to the Muslim castle, looking north and northeast, the directions of entry into Madrid through the river. A Christian castle was there in the twelfth century and a hunting lodge in the fourteenth and fifteenth centuries. Rebuilt, improved, enlarged, and refurnished repeatedly by the Austrian dynasty, this building was the Royal Alcázar until the fire in 1734.

A new history began as a result of Felipe V's decisions to demolish the remains of the Alcázar and erect a new palace on the same site. Once the site was chosen and the concept formed of a new building that defined a dynasty proud of its legitimacy and desiring to reinforce it in everyone's eyes with a tangible, visible sign, only a renowned architect was needed to shape the royal will. This architect could come from either of the two art centers recognized by the Spanish Crown: France or Italy. Since the king was born at Versailles and the queen in Parma, an Italian was chosen. Filippo Juvarra (1678–1736) joined the priesthood when he was just over twenty years old, and he became famous in European courts as an artist, architect, and decorator while he was still very young. He was also a draftsman and renderer with a skilled, quick hand, a great creator of spaces and facades whose grandiose aspects he could express to his clients with precise strokes of the pencil.

Born in Messina in 1678, Juvarra was a Spanish subject, although this would have been irrelevant three hundred years ago. In 1703 he was in Rome, studying and working as an apprentice to the well-known master Carlo Fontana (1634–1714). During his stay in Rome, Juvarra created stage sets for Cardinal Pietro Ottoboni's theater in the Palazzo della Cancelleria. At this time he also knew Naples, with its outstanding examples of Italian Baroque art. His reputation expanded rapidly, and he received commissions for large funeral monuments, including those for Emperor Leopold I, in 1705, and for Pedro II of Portugal, in 1706. He also designed stage sets for the Teatro Zuccari of the queen of Poland, Maria Caszymira. Juvarra's most important promotion came in 1714, when at thirty-six years of age, he was retained by the Piedmontese court of Vittorio Amedeo II. He enriched Turin with some of his best buildings, among them San Filippo Neri (1715), Superga (1718), and the Palazzo Madama (1718).

Juvarra then traveled to Paris twice. There he met Robert de Cotte, Louis XIV's architect, and carefully studied Versailles and other French palaces, although it seems he was somewhat disappointed by Versailles. He had expected something grander and more "flamboyant," capable of carrying the glory of imperial Rome to the French court.

In 1719–1720 Juvarra was in Lisbon, summoned there by Joao II of Portugal, with the consent of the architect's major patron Vittorio Amedeo II of Savoy, to erect a great palace and basilica on the banks of the Tagus. The project's excessive size prevented its construction, but Juvarra left Lisbon well paid and honored by the Braganças. He then went on to London where he spent six months as a guest of the Portuguese ambassador to the British court, then under George I of Hannover.

Some scholars see in this English sojourn that Juvarra showed a certain taste for the architecture of Wren and Gibbs. Gibbs had been Juvarra's fellow-apprentice to Fontana in Rome. At any rate, Juvarra added the scenery of London and its environs to his already rich visual vocabulary, which he soon enlarged with visits to Holland, Paris again, and then back to Turin. He made other trips to Rome, and by 1735, still rather young but already an experienced and very talented architect, he had the highest credentials to design what was going to be the greatest European palace of its time. Before his short but fertile stay in Spain, Juvarra left two more superb samples of his worth in Turin: Stupinigi, begun in 1729, and the church of Il Carmine, in 1732.

With this background, Juvarra was clearly one of the best European architects to carry out a palace that the Spanish Bourbons could fully identify with and that would allow them to proclaim to all of Europe: "This is my house and my spirit."

King Felipe and Queen Isabel commissioned their ambassador in Rome, Cardinal Acquaviva, to endeavor (either in Rome or in Turin, now under Carlo Emmanuelle III, the son of Juvarra's patron Vittorio Amedeo II) to bring Juvarra to Spain for a projected three-year period to design the new palace.

Acquaviva was quick and successful, beginning his work in early January 1735 and obtaining the approval of the Savoyan king in

February of the same year. In April, Juvarra was in Spain and on April 12, 1735, he was introduced to the sovereigns in the Palace of Aranjuez where the Spanish royal family sojourned each spring. He began his feverish activity that same day. As a priest, he was unhindered by family life and duties that would prevent him from devoting himself fully to his new client. Felipe V, although younger in age, was ailing and mentally absent.

Some specialists believe that Juvarra may have brought some sketches with him to Spain for a huge palace and that he became discouraged after learning that there was not a large enough area of level land in Madrid to build it. Another source of disappointment was the king's insistence that he make the palace fit the site of the burnt Alcázar, which occupied no more than three or four hectares.

Juvarra's design was formidable, the top work of a mature, celebrated architect with a superb job record but eager to finally build the great regal complex that could not be built in Lisbon. But even though this could not happen in Madrid either, the Bourbons were going to taste their glory through the talent of the Sicilian priest.

But it is unlikely that Juvarra came to Spain with finished drawings. It seems more logical that before drawing a single line he would want to listen to the king and queen, as well as to all of the advisers and courtiers who would have provided him with what today is called a "program of requirements" specific to the Madrid court. What he must have had in mind since his departure from Italy was a visual image of the basic scheme of facades relevant to the new palace.

Juvarra worked tirelessly during the nine months he lived in Madrid. The palace design must have consumed a lot of time, but he still had the energy to do some of the drawings and give technical advice on the north facade of Aranjuez and the main facade of La Granja. Although he never saw even the start of La Granja, Juvarra's style can be seen in its layout and proportions. A comparison of the crowning of the main facades at Madrid and La Granja is a good exercise in architectural abstraction, and it substantiates the conclusion that there is a distant but very certain identity of style and language between the two designs.

These "minor" tasks for Aranjuez and La Granja as well as a design for the new Teatro de La Cruz in Madrid, are dwarfed by

Juvarra's almost total dedication to Madrid's New Palace. The project is huge as can be seen in the drawings preserved in Rome, probably copied by Francesco Sabbatini (1722–1797). Juvarra planned a large central courtyard, rounded corners on the north and south sides, and a great stairway on the western side, very much like that of the Palazzo Madama (and also like that of the Riofrío palace, which is in a minor key but fine and elegant).

This central courtyard was Baroque in shape and surrounded by three square courtyards at the west, north, and south. Together with other smaller ones they formed a T-shaped footprint. The whole was so large that, if built on the area occupied by the destroyed Alcázar, it would have extended on the west beyond the present Plaza de la Opera, the Plaza de la Armería, and the Almudena Cathedral to the south, and squeezed between the watersheds of what are now San Vicente and Segovia streets. Any future growth would have been impossible.

It was an oversized concept searching for a properly sized piece of property. Juvarra wanted to place the building in San Bernardino Heights, a flat hill where the Montaña barracks stood (home of one of Madrid's most famous regiments during this century, a site now occupied by the Egyptian temple of Debod); but this area was not large enough to contain Juvarra's design either if there were to be gardens around the palace.

The initial concept had highly elegant facades, their dadoes embellished with statues, a first floor with balustraded balconies, and an upper floor with simpler windows; both storys were unified by a gigantic row of double columns ending in Corinthian capitals. The whole was crowned with an architrave, a smooth frieze, and an impressive cornice supporting a continuous balustrade, interrupted only by the bases of the statues at the top. The central projections of the main facades, north and south, had five openings, and the secondary ones, east and west, only three. The arrangement of the facades strongly recalls the Palazzo Madama, but Juvarra gave it greater pomp and magnificence.

In summer and autumn of 1735 the king and the architect quarreled over Juvarra's beautiful, well-proportioned design, which any king might envy but that was too huge to build. In addition, Felipe insisted on building the new structure on top of the old alcazar to respect the magic and symbolism of a millenary site. The design had to be recast and considerably reduced in size, no matter how disappointed or adamant Juvarra was. So the Madrid Palace may be one of the few palaces in Spain, or in Europe, that instead of growing was shrunk from its inception.

The bitter dispute between the king and the architect, between the wish of the monarch to affirm the Bourbon stance yet respect the House of Austria and the superb plan drawn by the designer that ignored the physical constraints, was cut short by fate. By mid-January 1736, Filippo Juvarra fell sick, probably of pneumonia, retired to his home in the Calle Ancha de San Bernardo, and died within seven days, at the age of fifty-seven.

A new period opened with Juvarra's burial in the church of San Martín, not far from the Alcázar site that he had visited so often and studied in such detail. The architect was a victim of "deferred hopes," as an English traveler wrote. Yet, in little more than twenty years, the New Palace became a reality. Who could undertake that task, not with Juvarra's impractical plans, but following the aesthetic ideas of the dead architect?

Professor Francisco de la Plaza, of the University of Valladolid, who has studied the history of the palace, provides many clues to those years. The Marquis of Cerdeña, then the Spanish ambassador, stated in a harsh, definitive report that the ideal person to succeed Juvarra was his disciple Gianbattista Sacchetti (1696–1784). Although not brilliant, Sacchetti was an accomplished professional and knew his teacher's work well. In short, Sacchetti could be managed without much loss of the aesthetic pulse in Juvarra's drawings.

Sacchetti was from Turin, and he arrived in Spain at the age of forty, not as a young apprentice, as some writers contend. Nor had he been a child prodigy but instead a hard worker who learned slowly. He was persistent, thorough, but extremely timid and not at all ambitious. These qualities were the key to his appointment, as Cerdeña has accurately noted. But despite his readiness to modify Juvarra's plans in order to make a viable palace, Sacchetti's life in Madrid was not easy. From the first months of his stay, he experienced the war against him by the Marquis de Scotti, Queen Isabel's adviser and a strong influence

at the court. The marquis was intent on making the ideas of another architect prevail, those of his protegé Virgilio Rabaglio (1711–1811), who in turn followed the marquis' ideas. When Sacchetti arrived in 1736, there was no longer any argument about the site. The royal decision was very firm. The revised drawings were completed in little more than six months. On April 6, 1738, with the site already cleared and prepared and the first agreements with the contractor executed, the first stone was laid in the center of the south facade, about eleven meters below the present level of the Plaza de la Armería.

This was the opportunity of Sacchetti's lifetime. On Juvarra's groundwork, he placed all his ability and experience as architect, builder, and engineer. Indeed, Sacchetti had joined the Madrid court as a hydraulic engineer, with the title of Master Fountain Builder for the Village of Madrid, and his first commission was to build a fountain.

To design the palace and manage the construction site was not an easy job, but Sacchetti had a good assistant and excellent draftsman in Ventura Rodríguez (1717–1785). Born in Cienpozuelos, a town near Madrid, Rodríguez later became a distinguished architect. Court intrigues never ceased around Sacchetti, and his designs were always compared with those of other architects who were not necessarily better but who had the backing to obtain projects. Palace construction took about twenty years and was an enormous financial undertaking, but, as the French ambassador commented, Felipe V was the most powerful and therefore the richest monarch on earth. Workers toiled by the thousands, moving about under "an impeccable organization with a solid administrative framework, with all sorts of subordinates and offices, the whole integrated in a very well-structured, pyramidal hierarchy, from the architect Sacchetti and his assistants down to the last teams of stonecutters and masons, in a clear, exemplary sequence." Professor de la Plaza adds to this that "there was also a clear separation between Spanish and Italian craftsmen and, since these [the Italians] were as a rule more able, they enjoyed certain advantages. The work took place in a huge fenced-in enclosure, with eight gates and the workshops and different jobs were well distributed within it. The hierarchy, discipline, efficiency, and rapid pace at the site could be compared with the last stages of work at El Escorial."

Over five hundred files are kept in the Obras Palacio (Palace Construction) section of the Palace Archives, but very few specialists have studied them thoroughly. Studies by Chueca, Tamayo, Kubler, Fernández de los Ríos, or Bottineau are good on the whole, but they only scratch the surface. A new generation of scholars, headed by Jörg Garms, José Luis Sancho Gaspar, Delfín Rodríguez Ruiz, and a few others, seems to have taken the torch from their predecessors, and they continue to work on a palace that has acquired certain popularity only in the last three decades. It is hard to understand how a palace that Rome and Paris would be proud of could remain almost forgotten for two centuries. Perhaps the same thing has happened to the workshops themselves, but we know now that they were a veritable school of building trades.

Researcher José Luis Sancho, the person who knows most about many aspects of the palace, states that "the organization of the palace workshops . . . can be taken as a model. It was a strong attraction for specialized Italian craftsmen, as well as a training center for Spanish workers, and certainly a *school* where the definition of an official late Baroque classicist architecture took shape. Ventura Rodríguez, Hermosilla, Diego and Juan de Villanueva . . . were trained in this *palace school*, which in a strict sense was the origin of the Academia de Bellas Artes de San Fernando."

Any construction workshop that lasts twenty years, aside from struggling against many external factors, has to struggle against itself, like any creative process. The Madrid palace workshop had to cope with dozens of competing designs and many conflicting opinions among hostile court circles. The job progressed relatively fast in spite of its magnitude and complexity—it encompassed many thousand square meters—as well as Sacchetti's modifications of his drawings as the work progressed.

The basic construction lasted seventeen years, from 1738 to 1755, and it was ten more years before the palace could be considered completely finished and habitable. The basements were built in four years of intense labor, up to approximately the present level of Plaza de la Armería, along with foundations, extraordinarily thick retention walls, vaults, skylights, wells, and sanitation works. These were all a truly masterful achievement of the stonemasons and the brick makers, who molded and fired the clay blocks to the exact shapes required by the bricklayers. The next four years were devoted to building the ground floor, with its prominent bossed-granite facade, main entrances, stairways, and rooms vaulted in very diverse techniques. Two years later, by the end of 1746, the main story could be considered finished. Felipe V had already died and Sacchetti now had a new boss, Felipe's son King Fernando VI, who reigned from 1746 to 1759. About 1749, according to José Luis Sancho, "The entire west side was ready to be roofed temporarily, because at that time King Fernando and Queen Bárbara de Braganza were thinking of occupying the lower floor."

Once the main construction was finished, interior decoration followed as well as the wings extending north and south from the square main structure. The wings had to take these directions since the east side was very close to city houses, and because of the contour of the land to the west any extension had to be ten or twelve meters below the ground floor. In 1749 Sacchetti, his capacity more than proven and tested, had to fight a new battle. In addition to the counterproposals he contested in 1736, still more proposals, ideas and sketches arose from Arce, Galve, Ribera, de Cotte, Fuga, Carnevari, Bonavia, and many others. There were even attempts to call a competition. Sacchetti envisioned his work subjected to further opinions on minor changes and possibly even extensions, but in 1750 the building was a reality.

Sacchetti had faithfully interpreted the ideas of Juvarra and built a palace that could claim to be a direct descendant of the Royal Palace of Messina, designed by Juvarra in 1714 for his first grand patron, Vittorio Amedeo II. But the New Palace, as it was known in Madrid during its first century, had another aesthetic look that was even stronger if possible than the Sicilian palace. Sacchetti's palace resembled the Palazzo Chigi-Odescalchi designed by Giacomo della Porta and Carlo Maderno in the sixteenth century and altered by Gianlorenzo Bernini (1598–1680) in the seventeenth century. In this way, first Juvarra, and more properly Sacchetti afterward, introduced Bernini's style in Madrid, a style well known to both from their stays in Rome. Bernini's presence in Madrid is visible in certain windows, adornments, and layouts that were very successful in Rome. This was the big cultural news in mid-eighteenth-century Madrid.

This Sacchetti-Bernini, or Madrid-Rome, relationship via the model of the Palazzo Chigi-Odescalchi is a point that Professor Fernando Chueca defends even more strongly. In the idiom of the Madrid palace he sees a faithful, elegant, more advanced reinterpretation (and, we believe, better constructed) of the Bernini palace. Indeed, the scheme of the east and west facades of the Madrid palace is very much like that of the Chigi-Odescalchi elevations: a base course, double windows with svelte mullions and a finial atop an elegant little roof; a lower row of smaller windows has two well-designed brackets at either side. Above, on the main story, the windows have alternating triangular and curved Romanate pediments. On the second story, the windows are less ornamented. These two levels are linked on the facade by pilasters with composite capitals that support the architrave. Above this is a forceful frieze adorned with elegant modillions; a wide cantilevered cornice bears the balustraded parapet.

This is no less than Bernini's Roman design of about 1664, but his was topped by graceful sculptures on the facade pilasters. Bernini solved the problem of superposed storys with great skill in a Baroque idiom with clear classical roots. Indeed, the problem had been addressed in Italian secular architecture almost two centuries earlier, in the Florentine palaces of the Medici-Riccardi and the Strozzi, by Michelozzo and Benedetto da Maiano respectively. But the Berninian facades show a more advanced and successful formulation in a restrained Baroque language. It seems to this writer, however, that the most perfect example in eighteenth-century Europe is Madrid's Royal Palace for the following reasons: the quality of its construction, its style and proportions, the wise choice and combination of materials with their particular textures and colors, and the variations from the basic scheme of the Odescalchi that the Madrid palace employs to resolve its own site problems.

Sacchetti's floor plan for the Madrid palace has the extremely refined but typical shape of a medieval French castle: an almost square structure around a square courtyard, with setoffs in the outer corners suggesting towers. Sacchetti, just as Juvarra would have, oriented the four facades to the cardinal points of the compass. The drift of the north facade relative to the geographic north is minimal,

unlike El Escorial where the displacement of the facades is visible and intentional.

The south facade of the Madrid palace is the main one, with its finely designed access to the building. This is the king's entrance, facing the sun as did the main facade of the old Alcázar. The east, or *oriente*, facade, gave its name to the city plaza built on that side of the palace in the nineteenth century. At its center is the secondary access, or prince's entrance, and given the layout of Madrid this entrance is used most often. And the facade itself is the best known and celebrated, because it can be seen better from the city streets.

The lower levels of the south and east facades are the same height, as are upper levels of these facades, recalling the Palazzo Odescalchi, although the Madrid palace facades are superior in both conception and proportions. Sacchetti planned an excellent treatment using horizontal bands of granite across the lower level and tall, narrow windows in the Roman manner, framed in limestone and with the same Berninian cowl. This level also has low windows, flanked by two limestone brackets, for providing daylight to the first basement. There are small openings above the cowls, again for daylight where the lower floor does not reach the full height of the exterior level, thus a mezzanine is created. This solution multiplies the potential uses of the interior space and enriches the exterior composition.

The ground floor facade ends with a strong limestone band, and the main story is much more generous in height. But instead of a single row of windows, the facades offer a new element: little windows between those of the main and the second storys, a deviation from the Bernini scheme described above. These little windows are fake in some cases and therefore merely for compositional effect; but when they are not, they let the daylight in and create a second mezzanine. The second story windows are also trimmed with limestone but the design is much more restrained.

These three levels of fenestration are unified by gigantic Tuscan pilasters and composite columns, Michelangelo's solution handled masterfully by Sacchetti with a unique richness of proportions that ennobles the entire building. This main structure, from the base to the architrave, far from being flat and monotonous, offers a variety of light and shadow in an interlocking pattern. It is a display of the best architecture that was practiced in Europe at the time. As in the Roman palace, the graceful windows of the main story have alternately triangular and curved pediments.

When Le Corbusier some fifty years ago made the exaggeration that architecture is just a play of light and shadow, he was obviously not thinking of the facade in Madrid. Many of his followers, however, recall his comment when they analyze the texture, smoothness, and plasticity of stone that create strong aesthetic emotions.

At the top of the palace is a simple limestone architrave and a smooth unadorned granite frieze. And the forceful limestone cornice extends out a meter and a half without brackets by means of powerful binding stones. Another level above is hidden by the band supporting the block-and-baluster parapet. Sacchetti topped the solid blocks of the parapet with statues, in a clear Berninian manner, but Carlos III had them removed.

Thus, into a two-part scheme six levels were fitted; ground floor, first mezzanine, main story, second mezzanine, second story, and attic, this last wisely hidden behind the base of the balustrade. A masterful way to clothe a six-level building (seven if the windows that let daylight into the first basement are included) with a Baroque language that constantly recalls classicism.

Sacchetti's ability as a builder is evident in the north and west facades too, where he had to adapt this simple classical scheme to the drop imposed by the topography. The north front follows the plan described above, but the granite base of the facade is extended downward. The exterior level so created corresponds to the first basement, and to this a gentle slope was added for both static strength and aesthetics. A terrace in front of this first basement converts it into a ground floor. Another terrace occurs in this facade at the second basement level, since the drop here is more pronounced. (The royal stables are now located in this second basement.) The solution for the west facade was even more difficult, since the contour is even steeper. This problem was solved in the second half of the 1750s by Ventura Rodríguez, who designed a system of half-basements, retaining walls, and ramps in the finest carefree Baroque style. This style can be seen in the great facade of the Camellia Greenhouse.

Thus, the Royal Palace of Madrid was conceived with a simple and beautiful basic scheme, a scheme that was adapted to a difficult terrain in order to enclose huge, complex interiors. From a strictly architectural viewpoint, the solution is perfect. Very difficult problems are resolved with a clean plan, without loss of beauty and without distorting the primary architectural elements. The palace has a coherence, a unity that among other Spanish palaces is only found in El Escorial.

After examining the vertical aspect of the facades, it is useful to look at the horizontal components. Although the stone mass of the palace presents a homogeneous, static, majestic appearance, its four facades are not identical. The east front has projections at both ends that suggest nonexistent towers and another in the center, the balcony of the Everyday Dining Room. The openings follow a 3 - 6 - 3 - 6 - 3 scheme. That is, there is a total of 21 openings, three each for the three setoffs and six each for the two intermediate walls. The pilasters of the "6" zones are of the Tuscan order and those of the "3" are fluted columns almost independent of the surface of the wall, which results in a chiaroscuro effect caused by the changes in plane.

The west facade presents the same 3 - 6 - 3 - 6 - 3 rhythm; but it is quite different from the east facade, since a lower level is added to accommodate the topography. This facade, from its lower point to the top, including the fantastic "incognito stairway," the greenhouse, and the broad landscaped footing, measures almost seventy meters in height. It is worth descending to the Paseo de la Virgen del Puerto to contemplate the magnitude of this facade full of architectural suggestions, along with the gardens and fountains of Campo del Moro.

The south or main facade is different too, with a change of rhythm to 3 - 1+5 - 3 - 1+5 - 3. This is because one of the six windows in each intermediate wall is set out with a composite column to signal the king's entrance. The north facade, aside from gaining two levels down with two terraces, does not have the 3 - 6 - 3 - 6 - 3 formula either but is arranged instead as 3 - 5 - 5 - 5 - 3, since the central section is widened to incorporate the Royal Chapel. The quasi-rectangular volume of the palace is broken only by the half-sphere of the chapel dome on the north side. This is a clear concession to the symbolism required by the ceremonial christening of the royal heir.

This use of the dome comes from a very old tradition in Spanish architecture. Many other traditions associate the dome with the de facto power of the king. It is placed, for example, above the throne hall in the Muslim *qubbas*, or over Felipe II's Paço da Ribeira tower in Lisbon. But the dome of the Royal Palace of Madrid is a power symbol for the future king who will be baptized under a replica of the celestial vault. Sacchetti understood the duality of architecture and symbology well, but the Marquis of Scotti did not. Consequently, his faithful Rabaglio designed a small elliptical chapel for the Riofrío palace, without a dome, and without the spatial charm of the Madrid palace, which he could have taken as a model.

The main stairway from the lobby to the first story was planned by Sacchetti as a double stairway. If his drawings had been executed, Madrid would have had an immense, double, imperial stairway that would best that of the Palazzo Madama. But Carlos III decided against the double stairway, so that he could have another hall, the famous Hall of Columns, where many official functions are held.

Despite this mutilation, the single stairway is impressive, with treads of single pieces of stone seven meters long. After the landing, the stairway is divided into two stretches to reach the first floor under the fantastic dome lit by oculi and painted by Corrado Giaquinto (1700–1765) with a fresco titled *The Triumph of Religion and the Church.* In this awesome space the usurper King of Spain José I received his brother Napoleon Bonaparte during the emperor's brief visit to Madrid. Napoleon climbed the stairs in silence up to the landing, where he stopped and said, *"Vous serez mieux logé que moi."* And then, with his hand on one of the marble lions, he exclaimed, *"Je la tiens enfin, cette Espagne si désirée."* This may be more legend than historical fact, but the scenery justifies the fantasy.

The principal rooms, apart from the grand stairway, are located in the south wing of the palace. These spaces constitute what may be called the "official palace," and they include the Salon of the Halberdiers, used by this royal guard unit until it was disbanded by the Republic on April 14, 1931. One outstanding hall in this southern wing is the Salon of Columns, which replaced what would have been the other side of a double stairway. Today lectures and concerts are held here, often with the king and the queen in attendance. In this grand hall, presided over by the bronze statue of *Carlos V Defeating Fury*, the Treaty of Accession of Spain to the European Community was signed on June 12, 1985. Carpets, tapestries, lamps, gilded moldings and garlands, and the ceiling painting *The Birth of the Sun* by Corrado Giaquinto (1700–1765) complement the walls of Colmenar stone.

The most famous room in the south wing is the Throne Room, and it extends along five windows of the facade. Also called Besamanos (Royal Audience Hall) or Reinos (Hall of Kingdoms), this is the most elaborately decorated room in the palace, with mirrors, console tables, lamps, and bronzes. A painting by Giovanni Battista Tiepolo (1696–1770) on the vault has given the room its special character forever. The recently restored velvet linings give new splendor to this hall whose back wall was erected where the main facade of the old Alcázar once stood.

The series of three rooms named after the Italian decorator Matteo Gasparini (d. 1774) are among the most important in the palace. The second room, the Gasparini Antechamber, should be renamed the Goya Antechamber because four of Goya's paintings hang there. His two portraits of Carlos IV and two others of his consort Queen María Luisa are among the best paintings in the royal collection. If one were to choose a dozen pictures from the eight thousand in this collection, undoubtedly these four Goyas must be included. Another sensational painting in the palace is the polyptych, *The Lives of Christ and the Virgin,* by Juan de Flandes, the painter of Isabel the Catholic. The Salon Gasparini simply explodes, in its flooring and friezes as well as its walls. The lodgings in the southwest corner of Don Francisco de Asís, consort to Isabel II, can be seen from the Salon Gasparini, as one enters the west wing. The best rooms in this area are the one popularly called the *"Tranvía* (streetcar) *de Carlos III"* and the Salón de Tranvía where Carlos died. The Salón contains the king's portrait by Anton Raphael Mengs.

The Porcelain Room, next to the State Dining Room, is a small room with walls and ceiling covered in perfectly fitted porcelain panels that form a delicate green-on-white lattice. The State Dining Room is a grand stage for official banquets for as many as 130 guests. The room takes in all seven of the central windows of this wing, and it is in full use today. It was once made up of three smaller rooms where Queen María Amalia lived for a short time in the eighteenth century; the queen died a year after arriving in Spain from Naples. The Dining Room was first used for the wedding of Alfonso XII.

The other rooms on the way to the chapel are at present exhibition galleries for paintings, sculpture, silver, china, clocks, and musical instruments. Two small rooms next to the chapel house the reliquary and royal treasure. The latter contains the crown and scepter of the Spanish kings, which were last used when King Juan Carlos I was proclaimed King of Spain by the Spanish Parliament in 1975.

In the northwest corner are the lodgings of Queen María Cristina (1806–1878). The most famous room in the west wing is the Everyday Dining Room. It extends across the three central openings, with a long balcony known by some as Franco's Balcony because he addressed the crowd from it during three or four large demonstrations. Other rooms in this main building are the Salon of Mirrors, the Salon of Tapestries, the Hall of Arms, and the tapestry storage rooms as well as the Royal Chamber, where the king regularly receives foreign ambassadors.

The palace surrounds an almost square central courtyard of 50.87 by 50.42 meters. The facades of this courtyard are extremely interesting. They have nine openings on each floor, identical on the east and the west. The north and south facades are also identical to each other but vary slightly from those on the east and west. Although these too have nine openings, the one in the center is wider and the remaining eight narrower to accommodate the statues on the ground floor of four Roman emperors who were born in Spain: Trajan, Arcadius, Honorius, and Theodosius. Their roman vestments are replicated on two nearby stone statues, one of Carlos III at the foot of the main stairway and the other of Carlos IV on the landing.

The central courtyard has two levels. The open semicircular arches of the lower level form a portico, and the upper level arches are glazed and have rather compressed but eloquent little columns, in the manner of Sebastiano Serlio.

This almost square central building, 132 meters north to south and 129 meters east to west, is the great work Sacchetti managed to complete against all odds but that Carlos III disliked when he arrived in Spain. The king removed the white limestone balustrade statues of almost all the Spanish monarchs, beginning with the first Visigothic king, Ataulf. He kept only the statues of Felipe V and María Luisa, his parents, and those of Fernando IV and Bárbara, his stepbrother and stepsister-in-law, along with a few others on the plinth. The rest were scattered throughout Spain, and can be seen in Pamplona, Toledo, in Madrid's Retiro Park, and in the Plaza de Oriente in front of the palace.

Carlos III also eliminated one of the two main stairways and simplified the decoration as much as he could, trying to subdue a certain mannerism that did not please him. Not surprisingly, he also felt that the palace was too small. First, because it resulted from a drastic cut in Juvarra's plan, which reduced it to about one fifth its proposed size; and second, but not least, because Carlos III (who had been Carlo VII of Naples) had left half built the famous palace of Caserta, one of the largest European palaces of that time. The new king made decisions quickly. Ventura Rodríguez and Gianbattista Sacchetti were fired and replaced by Francesco Sabbatini. Giovanni Battista Tiepolo was replaced by Anton Raphael Mengs and the court was filled with Italian ministers, such as Grimaldi and the Marquis de Esquilache (Schilacci).

Sacchetti died in oblivion in 1784, and today he is the most unjustly forgotten of the architects who worked on the palace, even though what we see now is largely by his hand. Historically and culturally he was overshadowed by Juvarra and not a single exhibition, monograph, or doctoral thesis has been done on his work. Madrid owes to him its best building, but the city council has not named a street after him.

If the arrival of the Bohemian painter Anton Raphael Mengs (1728–1779), an artist very much to the taste of Carlos III, brought balance and academicism to the pictorial panorama of the court, the arrival of Francesco Sabbatini (1722–1797) did not equally influence building, primarily because of the lively and demanding personality of this Sicilian artist who was tirelessly active at the royal sites, enlarging the Palace of Aranjuez and more than doubling El Pardo. His most notable involvement in the Royal Palace of Madrid, however, was the so-called east extension, the same height as the rest of the palace and totally faithful to Sacchetti's construction in its shapes, materials, and proportions. This east wing is absolutely faithful to the whole complex, and it led to the creation of the future Plaza de la Armería, or parade grounds, completed later with two superb arcades during the time of Isabel II and Alfonso XIII.

If Sabbatini's feverish activity managed only to make the east wing a full reality, it was because of technical and economic obstacles. Sabbatini understood the projected expansion plans perfectly well, particularly the one Ventura Rodríguez had envisaged in 1758, and he planned another growth formula. Sabbatini projected two wings to the south, one to the east, which was built, and another to the west (never built), to create a large plaza on the south. But the most spectacular growth he envisaged was to the north. It was to be a large building complex with three courtyards, almost the size of the central one that was already finished, and a large nave aligned with the chapel in a way that would make the existing elliptical one only an access to the new temple. A drop in the contour of the land at the north of the palace made the price prohibitive, but the small part that was executed was very well integrated with the rest. In the first three decades of the twentieth century, King Alfonso XIII and Queen Victoria Eugenia resided on its first story.

The main changes in the nineteenth century, apart from interior redecoration and the new State Dining Room, were the enlarged arcades on the south close to the Plaza de la Armería, in line with Alfonso's thinking on restoration. A large expiatory temple was also planned, designed in Neo-Gothic style by the Marquis of Cubas. As a result, the large church planned by Sabbatini at the end of the eighteenth century, was becoming a reality—the crypt and the foundations were built at the end of the nineteenth century—but at the south side instead of the north, and in an aesthetic idiom far from Sabbatini's.

In the twentieth century only restoration and cleaning were carried out, mainly to repair the west facade, which was severely damaged by Franco's artillery during the 1936–1939 Civil War. The palace itself was not a military objective, but strongholds and magazines behind it ignited. Restoration work done in the 1940s and '50s was excellent. In the 1960s, an overall facade cleaning, restoration of the lead roof partly carried off during the Civil War to manufacture bullets, and removal of numerous fake chimneys added in the nineteenth century, returned the palace to its original appearance. The white limestone harmonizes with the gray granite, and when one arrives in Madrid from the west the white mass of the palace dominates the silhouette of the city.

Madrid's Royal Palace, like any palace, stemmed from the idea of a center of power, and it has been the political hub of Spain from 1760 to 1936. The Esquilache riots took place near its walls, as did the popular uprising against Napoleon's invasion in May 1808. French pillage during the Napoleonic war impaired some royal collections, particularly of the Armory, which was damaged again by a fire in 1884 (largely repaired and reopened in 1893). The common goal of all nineteenth-century insurrectional and supportive movements had the palace in Madrid as their goal.

Bullet marks are visible in the grand stairway from the shots fired when General Diego de León attempted to abduct Queen Isabel II who was then a young girl. The vaults painted by Maella, Mengs, and Tiepolo have witnessed political intrigues and conspiracies, cabinet meetings, and power crises. Prime Ministers Cánovas and Sagasta went to the palace to report to Queen Regent María Cristina and Canalejas reported to Alfonso XIII.

The *cuarto baxo* (lower floor) rooms on the west, intended as a residence for Fernando VI, became the office of the president of the Second Republic Don Niceto Alcalá Zamora from 1931 to 1936. In his memoirs Don Niceto said that "the Government prepared some rooms for us in what was the Royal Palace, now the National Palace . . . selecting those on the lower floor called the Prince's," meaning that the Republican regime recognized the palace as the main center of power and located the president's office and residence there, although Zamora never lived in the palace. General Franco, of course, went to the palace every week for thirty-five years to hold military and civil audiences and one Thursday a month to receive the credentials of foreign ambassadors.

Between Carlos III and Alfonso XIII, the Royal Palace was the home of the royal families of Carlos IV, Fernando VII, Isabel II, and Alfonso XII. The last royal family to live there, from 1906 to 1931, was that of Alfonso XIII and his wife, the British-born Victoria Eugenia (Ena) Battenberg, granddaughter of Queen Victoria. With the proclamation of the Republic in 1931, the palace lost its royal appellation until about 1970. General Franco preferred the name Palacio de Oriente, after the beautiful plaza on the east side of the building.

In the 1940s the palace was opened to the public as a museum to show the extraordinary collections of paintings, sculptures, clocks, fans, porcelains, and numerous objects of decorative art that had been kept there. This includes the tapestry collection, which in Alfonso XIII's time was only shown to the public on Holy Thursday. This collection is now housed in the palace, and some of the best tapestries can be seen daily.

The Royal Palace of Madrid today is a building with complex functions. Aside from its various museums, there are offices, workshops, and the Royal Guard Horse Stables; but it is used mainly for official ceremonies. King Don Juan Carlos I and Queen Doña Sofía with their unmarried children live in another, smaller palace near Madrid, La Zarzuela. Although the Royal Palace ceased to be a family residence in 1931, its surroundings and facades still evoke the same centuries-old emotions, and the building continues to be a superb setting for royal receptions. Foreign leaders received in the palace by King Juan Carlos with full dress ceremony, as was President Clinton, ascend the great stairway under the vault painted by Giaquinto and the walls lined with rich tapestries. These leaders are likely to feel the same awe that moved Napoleon when he came to visit his brother almost two centuries ago.

✠

The PALACE of EL PARDO

✠

The PALACE of EL PARDO

✠

The Royal Palace of El Pardo began with a sixteenth-century building that was doubled in size in the eighteenth century. But its origin is much earlier, dating to Fernando IV, king of Castilla and León from 1295 to 1312. The capture of Gibraltar by the Christians was the most important feat of his reign and a milestone of Castilian-Leonese policy in the early fourteenth century. The so-called Straight policy was to acquire the southern part of the peninsula in order to prevent a Moorish invasion from North Africa. Castilla had won the Guadalquivir River line and Aragón the Mediterranean flank, and the next step was to take the southernmost tip of the Iberian Peninsula in Gibraltar and Tarifa to provide Christian Spain with a deep rearguard and complete the long process of reconquest. Only a small enclave, the kingdom of Granada, remained in Muslim hands.

There are numerous fourteenth-century references to royal houses in the basins of large rivers or hunting grounds, far from the front lines. Among these are the buildings of Alfonso XI (1312–1350) and his son Pedro the Cruel (1334–1369), on the Sevillian banks of the Guadalquivir atop the old Moorish palace and the new Tordesillas palace by the Douro River that was soon turned into a monastery. In 1304, during the reign of Fernando IV, an "El Pardo house" is mentioned for the first time. This early building stood in the Dehesa Vieja, or Monte Hueco, and was most likely a small hunting pavilion in the middle of a thick forest with plentiful game.

Fifteenth-century references, from about 1470 to 1475, are clearer. They speak of a *"casa de plazer"* (recreation house), surrounded by oaks and junipers, where fêtes and hunting parties were held. It seems that the house, or fortress, was built by the Trastámara King Enrique IV (1425–1474) of Castilla and León. Here again the practice

occurs of carefully selecting the site before building. El Pardo was by a small stream, the Manzanares, surrounded by woods suitable for hunting and an hour's ride on horseback from the Alcázar of Madrid, nearer than Fernando IV's house in Segovia's Alcázar was to the hunting grounds of the Balsaín forest.

No drawings or plans remain of this fourteenth-century house, but from written descriptions and inventories we know it was more a castle than a palace, with at least three perimeter towers and a keep. The interior must have had various rooms, the *Salón rico* being the main room with the best views, like the one in Tordesillas built in the previous century. The enclosing walls were surrounded by a moat that was spanned by a drawbridge. Probably the moat was dry, since most castles in central Spain were built on high land far from a source of water.

El Pardo must have remained a castle until well into the sixteenth century, since there is little information about it during the reign of the Catholic kings. But we know El Pardo attracted the attention of Emperor Carlos V (Carlos I of Spain) perhaps because of its proximity to Madrid's Alcázar and most certainly because it was excellent for hunting, a sport the king enjoyed whenever his duties permitted. When Carlos set his eyes on El Pardo, he wanted to preserve and improve it, and in doing so the late Gothic castle was lost for the future. What did it look like? was it a trapezoid of about one hectare with corner towers, like the not-too-distant Manzanares el Real castle that still exists? was it similar to the aristocratic manors built by French or Flemish masters? or built in the more indigenous Mudéjar style? These questions cannot be answered, but the imperial will was to demolish the fortress and build a new royal house on the site. Why was it built in the same place if nothing was to remain of the old Castilian castle?

The explanation most likely lies in the absence of a culture of architectural preservation, which did not appear in the West until the eighteenth century, but what existed from time immemorial was a quasi-atavistic respect for the magic of places where ancestors had built their religious and courtly buildings. This trend emerged even before Roman times. The great English Gothic cathedral York Minister was built on the Saxon and Norman cathedral of Jorvik, and this in turn was built on the Roman basilica of Eboracum. The Louvre stands on the site of the Capetian château, the cathedral of Córdoba on the mosque, and the Royal Palace of Madrid on the medieval and Renaissance Alcázar. The Hapsburg dynasty's El Pardo had to be on the very site of the Trastámara fortress.

The construction process of the new sixteenth-century building is relatively well known. The building was designed in two L-shaped stages by the architect Luis de Vega (d. 1562). The north and west wings were built first and coexisted with the east and south wings of the old building, which were used as temporary lodgings until the first stage was completed. The floor plan is absolutely simple and rational; nothing was left to improvisational design or careless future enlargements by royal whim. The drawings in the archives of the Royal Palace in Madrid, probably the original drawings, show a small square alcazar with a rectangular central courtyard, and corner towers extending three meters in plan from the facades. It is a synthesis of the late medieval donjon geometry and a Renaissance residential palace that meets the requirements of courtly protocol and a new aesthetic language. Luis de Vega designed a square plan 54 by 54 meters with a double bay system on its four sides to allow a courtyard measuring 20 by 22 meters. The east and west wings have open galleries on the yard side, while the external facades of the north and south galleries are loggias.

The inner galleries, closed in the seventeenth century and reopened in 1989, are interesting. They are on two levels with eight arches each, which projects the central axis through a column. The Ionic columns are rather squat and the segmental arches supported by them are overly flattened, suggesting that De Vega probably had to match one of the heights of the old building. The connection between the arch and the Ionic capital is also striking. The entabla-ture boss is so narrow that it feels as if it is being compressed by the arches. Although the height of this lower floor may have been forced, the elevations of the inner arcades are well handled, and the almost five-century-old granite is practically intact. The upper floor is handsomer: dadoes with Burgundian coats of arms, balustrades, columns, and beautiful lintels form an expressive whole with the architrave, frieze, and cornice. This can be appreciated better since the galleries reopened after a recent restoration.

El Pardo's main entrance was on the west axis with an inscription carved in the granite: CAROLVS I ROM(anorum) IMP(erator) HISP(aniarum) REX, 1547, which is still visible today. Since the palace was built in two L's, its symmetry was on a diagonal axis. In fact, there are two diagonal stairways, one in the southwest corner of the courtyard and another in the northeast corner, suggesting that about 1547 only the northwest L was used, the wings reserved by protocol for the queen. One of the stairs led to the inner east gallery and to the north wing, with a nine-span exterior gallery, *la galería del cierzo* (gallery of the north wind), which was later closed because of the bitterly cold wind. The other L, the east and south wings containing the king's lodgings, was built in the second stage. The seven-arch gallery facing south was walled up for almost three centuries. It is not unusual that the queen's north gallery and the king's south gallery had nine and seven arches respectively, since an uneven number was the classic form when there was a central arch. But the even number of arches in the east and west interior galleries is rather striking, with the axis through a column.

This scheme is full of unique features, like L-shaped royal rooms, two diagonally opposed stairways, and one service stair beside each of the four towers, forming a sort of counter-tower within a highly precise geometry. The singularities are so numerous that it is difficult to clearly relate El Pardo to any European style. Some link it to the châteaus of the Loire, but this argument is weak, both culturally and formally. The central donjon of Chambord, the abstract scheme of Saumur, the main body of Chenonçeau, aside from the gallery, do not back this theory. The suggestion of an English or Flemish influence, through the then heir to the throne, Felipe, does not hold either, for chronological reasons. Another opinion holds that El Pardo is an evolution, a kind of updating of the old medieval fortress to a Renaissance villa. It is probably more accurate to fit El Pardo into the Spanish alcazar tradition, a square structure with corner towers, two internal and two external galleries, and certain Moorish traces, which are still alive in the mid-sixteenth century. Concessions to the old fortress, like the deep perimeter moat, can be observed. Although the moat had no water, it provided daylight and ventilation to the basement. Spanned by two bridges, the one on the west leading to the main gate, the moat is still preserved.

But the aspect of the new building, now a palace, had no similarity to the previous warlike castle. On the contrary, from the moat up it had a peaceful appearance with its low stone plinth and neatly bonded exposed-brick facades, which gave the whole building an ocher tone that blended perfectly with its background, the brown holm-oak forest.

The granite details were limited to window trimmings, richer on the main floor than elsewhere, and to the entrance gate. The magnificent imperial two-headed eagles visible today on the southwest and northeast towers are not seen in the seventeenth-century picture that hangs in El Escorial nor in the eighteenth-century view by Michel-Ange Houasse (1680–1730) in Riofrío. The Van der Berghe engraving of the Theatrum Hispaniae, however, shows them clearly. While the ocher facades blend well with the wooded backdrop, Felipe II's decision to roof the building in slate was an even happier choice. Now king, he wrote from Antwerp ordering the roofs of the Balsaín house to be covered with slate and then later ordered the same material for El Pardo.

On his return to Spain in 1559, Felipe's enormous impulse to build is clearly visible in his contributions to Balsaín, Aranjuez, the Alcázar, the Convent of the Descalzas Reales in Madrid, and of course El Pardo. In the 1560s he altered his father's idea of El Pardo somewhat by finishing the roofs and towers "in the Flemish manner." The Casa de Oficios (Services House) at the west of the palace, also was roofed in this way in 1563. A dense grove of trees extended from this building to the river bed, as Houasse's picture shows. Felipe also worked on the interior decoration of the palace relying on his architect Juan Bautista de Toledo (c. 1515–1567) until his death. By 1566

Gaspar de Vega (d. 1575), nephew of Luis, finished the four towers, leaving them ready to be covered with lead and slate. Among the alterations Felipe made to Luis de Vega's drawings, the Queen's Gallery and the framing of the opposing king's area remain. Many artists worked for the palace and within a few years made it a veritable painting gallery, just as El Escorial and the Alcázar in Madrid were becoming. It must have been delightful to stroll through the portrait gallery of El Pardo admiring the Titians and then contemplate the frescoes of Gaspar Becerra (1520?–1570), which are still preserved in the southwest tower. This corner is valuable for its original decorative elements. They have remained practically unchanged for four centuries, perhaps because the area was essentially closed during that time.

Felipe II decided not to build the proposed pavilion in front of the south facade, because it "would have made the house rather ugly." El Pardo was a royal residence and hunting base for more than a hundred years, a frequent stopover for the king on his way from the Alcázar to El Escorial through Galapagar. The route was later changed to Torrelodones, where Herrera prepared a modest house for brief stays by the royal family.

A fire broke out in El Pardo "on Saturday, March 3, 1604, one day after the king and the queen (Felipe III and Margarita) left for Madrid." The fire affected the roofs, a real forest of finely jointed pine timber arranged to enclose two attic levels, which can be inferred from an engraving by Van der Berghe. The damage was clearly extensive to construction elements, such as woodwork, wall surfaces, and slate, as well as stucco work, paintings, and tapestries.

Architect Juan Gómez de Mora (1586–1648) was charged with reconstructing El Pardo. His drawings in the Vatican Library and the Royal Palace of Madrid show how respectful his reconstruction was to the original design, including the moat that was slightly softened by curving the corners. Professor Virginia Tovar Marín, who is extremely knowledgeable about El Pardo and its environs, states that Gómez de Mora received a royal order to "return the building to its original state, and although he made some changes in the interior arrangement, they did not affect the architectural structure of the emperor's palace." Still, a doubt remains about whether the north wing was closed at the time of this reconstruction, as was always believed, or remained open throughout the seventeenth century, as Gómez de Mora's Vatican drawings indicate, and then was closed at the beginning of the eighteenth century.

El Pardo was a royal house through the seventeenth century, used primarily as a hunting or staging post on the way to El Escorial or Valladolid (capital of the kingdom for some years) but not a residence for the royal family for longer periods of time. No royal children were born there, which seems to affirm this. While El Pardo lacked the large halls required for weddings, christening ceremonies, and other receptions, some important events did take place there. Felipe IV (1605–1665) was married at El Pardo to his first wife, Isabel de Borbón, in 1615, but because they were both so young they had to wait five years to consummate their marriage. Isabel spent most of that time in El Pardo. In 1643 Felipe IV dismissed his favorite, the Count-Duke of Olivares, one of the most important and difficult decisions in his life. This had such implications that the king retired to El Pardo to ponder his grave political and personal crisis. Queen Isabel died in 1644, and Felipe IV sorrowfully retired again to El Pardo. He wrote to the Countess of Paredes de Nava, who had been the queen's lady in waiting: "I have lost a wife, an advisor, and a companion, and since I have not died of sorrow, I must be made of bronze."

The beginning of the 1640s was a bitter time for Felipe IV with waning power in Flanders, the Catalonian and Portuguese uprisings, the fall of Olivares, and the death of Queen Isabel. El Pardo was the scene or the backdrop of some of these events as well as of other happier ones. In 1649 Felipe IV spent a two-month honeymoon in El Pardo with his new bride and niece Mariana de Austria. The palace continued to be a site for brief stays and for hunting and riding. During an equestrian outing at El Pardo in 1689, Queen María Luisa de Orléans fell sick and was taken to the Alcázar, where she died five days later.

Two small but important buildings are within the same forest as El Pardo and near the palace: the Torre de la Parada and La Zarzuela. The Torre de la Parada dates from the sixteenth century. Because of his fondness for hunting Felipe II had it built before he became king. Designed by Luis de Vega, El Pardo's first architect, its style and color are very similar to those of El Pardo, with its granite plinth, bonded brick, flint panels, stone-trimmed windows, and slate-covered roofs and tower. Only a ruin remains today, but we know from seventeenth-century pictures that the building had two wings and a tower in between, with graceful brick chimneys and a spire. This was a mixture of the original seventeenth-century building and the additions ordered by Felipe IV, who converted it into a painting repository filled with the work of Peter Paul Rubens (1577–1640) and Diego Velázquez (1599–1660). The War of Succession in the early eighteenth century and the decoration of the Royal Palace in Madrid by mid-century put an end to the collection housed in the Torre de la Parada, a collection beloved by the two most art-minded kings of the Hapsburg dynasty.

La Zarzuela, near El Pardo, is the current residence of King Don Juan Carlos I and Queen Doña Sofia. This house was begun when the Infante Fernando, brother of Felipe IV, purchased land near El Pardo, by a little stream named Zarzuela, to build a country house surrounded by a park. But he was not able to see La Zarzuela completed. Fernando was born in El Escorial in 1609, made a cardinal when he was only ten years old, and is known to history as the Cardinal Infante Don Fernando. When he was scarcely twenty-three, he left Spain for a distinguished military and political career in Central Europe. Governor of Italy and Flanders, he commanded the Spanish army that together with the imperial forces under General Mathias Gallas defeated the Swedish in Nördlingen in 1634. Don Fernando died in Brussels at the age of thirty-two and was buried in El Escorial. Four splendid portraits of him hang in the Prado Museum. In one of them, by Velázquez, he wears hunting garb; in another, by Rubens, he rides horseback in battle. The other two are by Anthony Van Dyck (1599–1641) and Gaspar de Crayer (1584–1669).

The palace Don Fernando began was finished by his brother, Felipe IV, and it had an active life. Designed in the so-called Madrilenian Baroque style, it was the work of two outstanding architects, Juan Gómez de Mora, who drew the plans, and Alonso Carbonell (1590–1660), who executed them. A rectangular manor, it had five openings each on the front and back and seven on each side. Its predominantly brick facades had a stone plinth, stone window trimmings and cornice, and faintly suggested corner towers. Its slate roof has two rows of mansards. Lateral arched galleries enclose the gardens behind them, and there is a traditional central courtyard. A very popular and typically Spanish musical genre, a sort of light operetta, originated in the parties and balls given here and was named *zarzuela* after the palace.

A seventeenth-century gem in the eclectic but excellent Madrilenian Baroque style, La Zarzuela underwent the Wars of Succession (1701–1714), reforms in the nineteenth century, and heavy shelling during the 1936–1939 Civil War. The Madrid front cut through El Pardo, and the palace was used as an artillery observation post by the Republican army. Diego Méndez, the architect who rebuilt it in 1960, kept Gómez de Mora's basic layout but added a story by lowering the original main floor. Soon after Prince Juan Carlos married, in 1962, he made this building his family residence.

In the 1970s and '80s Manuel del Río designed several enlargements that converted La Zarzuela into a multifunctional complex, with reception halls and offices for the king, the queen, and their children, but its original master plan remains. The core is still that of the old seventeenth-century palace, but with a thoroughly modernized interior. A painting by Salvador Dalí (1904–1989) decorates the king's office and a sculpture by Eduardo Chillida (b. 1924) presides over the private garden. The halls are lined with fine portraits of members of the royal family over the last hundred years.

El Pardo, however, mother house of this group of forest buildings, inevitably underwent drastic reforms during the eighteenth century. A new dynasty brought a new style, but deeper changes were made toward the end of that century, when the Enlightenment and the revolutions in France and America brought new ways of thinking in politics and religion as well as in the arts. El Pardo in the late eighteenth century cannot be understood apart from the town that evolved around it and the profit-making productivity of the surrounding territory.

As a result of the first measures adopted by Felipe V (1683–1746), El Pardo ceased to be a hunting house with service buildings. By this time the area had begun to develop as an urban center. This also occurred in El Escorial, La Granja, and Aranjuez. Felipe V commissioned his architect, Francisco Antonio Carlier (1707–1750), to build a royal chapel between the palace and the Casa de Oficios. The king also made other alterations such as closing the inner galleries (now reopened) and modifying the spires, which lost their Flemish character and were given a more French look. Even the proportion of the towers was changed, by horizontal bands that divide them into four segments.

These variations were justified to some extent by the increased frequency of royal visits and events from the beginning of the eighteenth century. In 1714, Queen María Luisa Gabriela de Saboya, Felipe V's first wife, died in El Pardo, after a month's illness. A few months later at El Pardo, the widower king empowered Cardinal Acquaviva to arrange his second marriage to Isabel de Farnesio (Isabella Farnese). During his second period on the throne, after his son Luis's brief reign, Felipe continued the palace alterations. Carlier subdivided the Queen's Galleries and the Portrait Galleries with partition walls and made new rooms that altered the previously rigid scheme. The courtyard corners were beveled at the same time to allow shorter and more functional traffic paths from three angles, although the fourth was only decorative. Forty years later Sabbatini retained these in another remodeling but gave them a curved shape. Carlier also did the drawings for new dormer windows and a bridge to connect the main story of the palace with the choir of the new church.

In the first half of the eighteenth century another building was added to the complex: "La Quinta" de El Pardo, a recreation house owned by the Duke del Arco whose widow donated it to the king. The duke, who died in 1737, was the Master of the King's Horse and a close and loyal friend of Felipe. The sloping land around La Quinta was impeccably terraced with gardens. The property fell into relative disrepair after the 1868 revolution. From 1920 to 1930 it was occupied by the Prince of Asturias Don Alfonso, a topographer who also followed his avocations in agriculture and raising livestock. From 1931 the Republic deemed it a National Palace; on July 17, 1936, President Azaña was there on a brief holiday when news arrived of "a military revolt" in Morocco, which he initially considered unimportant. The building was restored in 1973, and Prince Juan Carlos used it to hold official audiences until Franco's death in 1975.

During his reign Felipe V had purchased land to enlarge the forest at El Pardo to 16,000 hectares, and in 1749 his son Fernando VI (1713–1759) ordered a wall built to enclose the property, with an entry gate on the road to Madrid's New Palace, then under construction.

The royal engineer Francisco Nangle received the king's order to build a handsome entry gate; Nangle in turn commissioned the sculptor Giovanni Domenico Olivieri to do the job. The gate was finished in 1753 and named the Puerta de la Venta del Corregidor, but it soon became known as the Puerta de Hierro (Iron Gate).

The arrival of Carlos III (1716–1778) to the throne on the death of his half-brother Fernando VI in 1759 meant a notable change in almost all of the palaces of the Spanish Crown. The east side of Madrid's Royal Palace was altered once more, redecorated, and enlarged. But this was only a fraction of what Carlos III envisaged. The Palace of Aranjuez grew to the west, with two wings that form its present "honor courtyard." Two small palaces were added to El Escorial for the Prince of Asturias and the Infante Don Gabriel. Naturally, El Pardo would not escape this drive toward architectural change. Carlos III had left behind a vast building program under construction in Caserta, not far from Naples. It was to have been the largest of all European palaces. With aesthetic ideas, good artists and builders, generous funds, and a sizeable family to house, Carlos was undaunted by a mere expansion campaign. So El Pardo, the hunting ground and palace, inexorably had to grow. The king purchased land from Alcobendas to Torrelondones and from Colmenar to Madrid, rounding off the efforts of his half-brother Fernando to achieve the large, walled enclosure that has lasted until today almost intact. In addition, Carlos doubled the size of the sixteenth-century palace. To this his faithful and efficient engineer, architect, and artist, the Palermo-born Francesco Sabbatini (1722–1797), applied his enormous entrepreneurial energies.

Sabbatini demolished the two east towers and converted the east facade into one side of a central courtyard to make it the new center line of symmetry for an added building identical to the old one. This form of growth is unusual, compared to the enlargement of Madrid and Aranjuez, but the modest size of El Pardo explains this, and adding new wings on the south side would have not been very useful. It is hard not to think about what Riofrío would be like if Carlos III and Sabbatini had turned their attention to it. No doubt they would have completed the *murallones* (the remains of the side wings), the parade ground, and the gardens. But the palace of the king's mother, Isabel, and stepbrother Luis Antonio remained unfinished.

Sabbatini worked at El Pardo from 1772 to 1776, but some of the finishing and decoration details were not completed until 1782. Enlarging and giving unity to so many different elements was a difficult architectural job, but Sabbatini achieved it in a masterly fashion. The works of architects Toledo, Luis and Gaspar de Vega, Gómez de Mora, and Carlier, of artists such as Caxes, Cabrera, Castello, and Becerra, and of many craftsmen who worked over two centuries at El Pardo were evident in the final result. Their work mixed with that of new artists: Juan Antonio Rivera, Zacarías Gonzáles Velázquez, Bartolomeo Rusca, Gaetano Pisarello, Pierre and Robert Michel, José del Castillo, Francisco Bayeu, and Francisco Goya. These treasures were enclosed in a rectangle of 118 by 55 meters, with towers in its four corners and two setoff volumes marking the axes and the north and south entrances. The building is arranged around three courtyards that were named in the twentieth century: Patio de los Austrias, Patio Central, and Patio de los Borbones. The American Hispanist George Kubler writes that El Pardo "combines French, German, and Italian forms but the whole is unmistakably Hispanic."

In this expanded setting, embellished with new landscaping and with more theatrical and ample proportions, Sabbatini could easily accommodate the four areas required by court ceremonial on the main floor: the salons of Carlos III, which more or less coincide with those of Felipe II, and the central section of the main area, composed of the king's dining room and oratory. Sabbatini placed the quarters of the Prince of Asturias, the future Carlos IV, in the southwest L of the new building and those of the infantas diagonally opposite. And finally, on the east side of the old building, are the quarters of the Infanta María Josefa Carmela, with access through the old stairway used by Queen Margarita de Austria (1480–1530) at the beginning of the sixteenth century.

Young Goya painted the designs for the tapestries the Royal Tapestry Workshop wove to decorate El Escorial and El Pardo. Goya worked in two phases, the first, in 1775, resulted in nine hunting scenes designed for El Escorial and the second, in 1776–1778, included ten scenes for the Prince's Dining Room in El Pardo.

Designed to the wishes of Carlos III and completed by Carlos IV (1748–1819), the palace was extended and redecorated to last over two more centuries, and most of it is preserved today. The eighteenth-century palace concept as a residence for the royal family and close relatives began with Felipe V, who prolonged his stays at El Pardo and Aranjuez, but the palace became much more under Carlos III and Carlos IV. The four-area layout of El Pardo explains this. Carlos III reserved just a fifth of the main floor for himself and gave larger portion to Prince Carlos and Princess María Luisa. The northeast corner was for his granddaughters, the infantas Carlota Joaquina, María Amalia, and María Luisa Vicenta, and the west wing for his malformed daughter, Infanta María Josefa Carmela, popularly nicknamed *La Pepa*. In Goya's famous portrait *The Family of Carlos IV*, the infanta is at the viewer's left with a patch on her temple, between the Prince of Asturias Fernando and the Infanta Carlota Joaquina. It is easy to appreciate the presence of the family structure in the enlargement of El Pardo Palace as well as the passion that Carlos III felt for hunting. The king went hunting almost every day, and El Pardo was less than two leagues from the palace in Madrid.

In the 1770s and the '80s, Juan de Villanueva (1739–1811), a young architect trained in Rome, began to work at El Pardo. Between 1772 and 1774 he designed a little house situated at the back of the palace with direct access from the north gate, called "a country house for His Highness." Near the stairway of the prince's room, this allowed young Carlos to go in and out readily. The house had painted vaults and it was surrounded by a boxwood garden. Despite the abundant documentation, there are doubts about the chronology of its construction. Researcher José Luis Sancho has found evidence that Villanueva worked on it again in the late 1780s. What is interesting is that, as Fernando Chueca points out, *La Casita del Príncipe* (the Prince's Little House) is the work of a mature architect, and no less valuable for its size. Its five-part design, with the central and end volumes higher than the two intermediate wings, creates a pleasant arrangement. Professor Carlos de Sambricio sees an echo of Palladio in the axes of the house. The delicate, sensitive overall design cannot be appreciated fully today because of the mutilated east and west gardens. The rooms overlooking the west garden were unabashedly open, while those facing the east were more modestly shielded. The excellent interiors are still as they were originally designed, making

the house a testimony to the architectural and decorative taste of two centuries ago. Unfortunately, the gardens are difficult to reconstruct, tangled as they are in a maze of highways, conflicting interests, and red tape. But this difficulty stems mainly from the misplaced development of El Pardo in the twentieth century.

El Pardo Palace was almost untouched in the nineteenth century. Carlos III's plan was valid for his successors who did not alter the main halls. González Velázquez, however, redecorated the theater at the end of the time of Fernando VII and painted some of the vaults of the king's lodgings on the south side. The walls and ceilings of these rooms are interesting, but the great hidden treasures are the murals by Gaspar Becerra (1520?–1570) in the southwest turret. Painted over four centuries ago, they are awaiting restoration.

Some memorable historic events took place in El Pardo after the restoration of the monarchy in 1874. Alfonso XII (1857–1885), who knew the palace well from his hunting in its forest, decided to lodge his future wife there. María Cristina de Habsburgo, and her official and family retinue, arrived in Madrid on November 23, 1879, six days before the wedding. So El Pardo went back to its old function as prenuptial royal hotel, which it had been for Isabel de Borbón in the sixteenth century. Alfonso XII died in El Pardo on November 25, 1885. He was taken there some days earlier by physicians's orders, in secret to avoid alarming the people. Queen María Cristina honored his dying words by maintaining the balance between the vying conservative (Cánovas) and liberal (Sagasta) forces who signed the Pact of El Pardo on the eve of the king's death. Alfonso died in the room designed by Sabbatini for the Prince of Asturias. It was converted thirteen years later by the Queen Regent María Cristina into a simple oratory with a Neo-Gothic altar with two superb ivory carvings, a sixteenth-century crucifix, and an eighteenth-century sculpture of the Virgin.

Alfonso XIII (1886–1941), following in his father's footsteps, lodged his bride, Victoria Eugenia (Ena) of Battenberg, in El Pardo, from her arrival in Madrid on May 25, 1906, until their wedding on the last day of that month. The civil marriage was performed in the Salon of the Ambassadors, known now as the Goya Salon because the artist designed the tapestries that decorate it. The marriage certificate was signed on the same Empire-style mahogany table with gilded swan legs on which, twenty-seven years earlier, Alfonso XII and María Cristina had signed theirs. The ceremony was witnessed by the Prince of Wales, later George V; by Archduke Francisco Fernando, whose assassination eight years later in Sarajevo precipitated World War I; the Russian czar's uncle Vladimir; Kaiser Wilhelm's brother Heinrich; and a young United States Army officer, grandson and namesake of Ulysses Grant, the American general and president on whose tomb the Infanta Eulalia had placed a bouquet of flowers in 1892. The infanta reminded the young Grant that his grandfather had been received by Alfonso XII in El Pardo as head of an American delegation. On a visit to Madrid, French President Raymond Poincaré stayed in El Pardo as a guest of Alfonso XIII, and the last European empress, Zita of Hapsburg, stayed there after her husband Karl IV died in 1921.

El Pardo's very rich history becomes increasingly better known and more exact in our own time. The Spanish Civil War of 1936–1939 radically changed the condition of the palace, when it became a barracks for Republican troops. The great Spanish poet Rafael Alberti recalled his stay there: "I lived in El Pardo Palace for some weeks, at the end of 1936, the gravest moments of the defense of Madrid. General Kebler's XI International Brigade headquarters were there. We celebrated a 'wartime Christmas party' in El Pardo that year, attended by the commanders of the Madrid forces, such as Lister, the Garibaldian Paciardi, Gustavo Durán, and many others. It was a palace, but it had the inevitable atmosphere of a barracks, underneath the vaults painted by Bayeu and the tapestries of Téniers and Goya."

None of those generals could imagine that their enemy, General Franco, would celebrate Christmas in that same palace in 1940. The royal palaces were undoubtedly symbols of the state. In the same way that the emerging Republic made them official residences for the president in 1931, General Franco commissioned his architect Diego Méndez to restore El Pardo for his role as head of the state. Franco lived in El Pardo for thirty-five years, until his death in 1975, but so little maintenance was done during that time that the basements were reduced to squalid warehouses. Several generations of Spaniards associate El Pardo with Franco's regime, not only as a hermetic, distant palace but also as the symbol of his rule, forgetting that it had been a famous site for almost seven centuries.

Franco installed his office in Carlos III's dining room to hold audiences and receive visitors. The walls of this room are decorated with the portrait of Isabel the Catholic by Juan de Flandes and Brussels tapestries depicting the battles of Archduke Alberto (husband of Felipe II's daughter Isabel Clara Eugenia and co-governor of Flanders). On its ceiling is Bayeu's fresco the *Apotheosis of the Spanish Monarchy*. Franco kept only a few photographs and souvenirs, surrounded by piles of papers and files, on his desk. His adjacent work room was much smaller, only twelve meters square. This had been the oratory of Carlos III. Although it was refloored in the 1940s with industrial tiles, the ceiling fresco remains.

When Eva Perón visited Madrid in summer 1947, Franco showed his gratitude to Argentina for assisting Spain by ordering immediate restoration of rooms to house her in the northwest corner of his own El Pardo residence (next to the old quarters of Infanta María Josefa). From 1953, foreign dignitaries have stayed in La Moncloa Palace, which was reduced to shambles during the Civil War and restored in the manner of Carlos IV.

El Pardo was opened as a museum in 1977, but this lasted only a year. When President Adolfo Suárez installed the residence and offices of the head of the government in La Moncloa, the state was left without a place to lodge foreign dignitaries. This function was transferred temporarily to the Palace of Aranjuez, until 1983, after El Pardo had been restored and provided with first-class hotel accommodations. Since then monarchs, presidents, and many other illustrious visitors have honored El Pardo with their presence. In 1983 the poet Alberti set foot again in the palace, forty-seven years after that "war Christmas party," this time as a guest at a reception for the king and queen of Sweden. Alberti asked whether "those marvelous Goya tapestries were still there." The answer, of course, was yes!

The PALACE of EL ESCORIAL

The PALACE of EL ESCORIAL

✠

Few visitors to El Escorial expect to find a typical Bourbon palace adorned with tapestries, gold, and clocks and full of color and gilded moldings in the style of Carlos IV, a style in vogue by the late eighteenth century. The word monastery usually precedes the name of El Escorial, and indeed it first housed the Hieronymite order. This and its basilica, libraries, gardens, and pantheon all tend to mask the palace. But the palace itself is a very important and interesting component of El Escorial. Its initial design is by Juan Bautista de Toledo (c. 1515–1567), who worked under the watchful eye of his patron Felipe II (1527–1598).

The origin of the palace of El Escorial is thus connected to the idea of a monastery, but from the start it was intended to be more than a monastery. A building of its complexity required a long period of planning by the king and his assistants regarding both its design and its location. When Felipe II appointed Toledo royal architect on July 15, 1559, the king took the first of a series of actions that eventually led to the construction of the colossus of El Escorial.

At this time, Felipe II was thirty-two years old, twice widowed, well acquainted with Italy, France, England, and Flanders, and possessed of a humanistic, artistic, and mathematical education uncommon in a man of such power. But, as the symbol of a Catholic monarchy ruling by divine right, he believed that his power came from God and from his beloved father Carlos I (1500–1558; Holy Roman Emperor Charles V, 1519–1558). The emperor had abdicated, leaving Felipe most of his possessions, and then retired to a remote monastery in Extremadura to die. In just three years, starting in 1559, many circumstances and events came together in Felipe II's life and many of his wishes became actuality.

Felipe II had vowed to build a pantheon worthy of his parents' imperial dignity, one that would perpetuate their memory with a tangible expression of his sincere filial love. It was not to be erected in Innsbruck, where father and son might have talked of situating it eleven years earlier, as they navigated up the Rhine to Flanders. Nor was the Royal Chapel of Granada the right location, because of the priorities of Felipe's parents and grandparents. Nor was the Chapel of the New Kings in Toledo the proper place for a new dynasty. Felipe II had to link a new pantheon to a religious building, a great human work that symbolized the aims and aspirations of his complex life. His rational, syncretic personality was to take physical form in a monastic building housing a tomb for his parents, himself, and his nearest relatives.

The year 1561 was crucial. During that year the king moved the court from Toledo to Madrid, the city that became the capital of the kingdom from that time on (except for a brief period in Valladolid, from 1601 to 1607). Felipe was already entertaining the idea of a great monastery with a royal burial place. In the old Spanish tradition, this was to be combined with a royal palace—a center of power where he could live, pray, tend to state affairs, and carry on a family life.

With the court now settled in Madrid and the great admiration the king felt for highly geometric schemes and central axes, the site of El Escorial was a natural choice for his grand political and religious monument. It seems that a committee, made up of physicians, philosophers, and architects, including the architect Toledo, spent several months studying a number of options for submission to the king: Manzanares el Real, La Fresneda, La Alberquilla, and El Escorial itself, the first three close to the present monastery, and the Guisando area near a Hieronymite monastery that today is in ruins.

The king chose El Escorial. Then a part of Segovia, in the district of Casarrubios, the land included the oat fields of Fuentelámparas, the farms and hamlets of Campillo, and La Fresneda monastery. It was the ideal site, on a gentle slope at the foot of Mount Abantos, less than a half day's journey from El Pardo, El Bosque, or the alcazars of Segovia and Madrid.

There was no doubt that the Hieronymite friars would be in charge of the monastery, since this order had a long Hispanic tradition and strong ties with the Crown. Felipe II frequented the church of San Jerónimo el Real in Madrid and his father died in the Hieronymite monastery of Yuste.

Juan Bautista de Toledo received the commission to design the building in August 1561, and by spring 1562 the first plans for the complex, the *traza universal* or general plan, had taken shape. This was essential, because very dissimilar spaces were put together to facilitate interior functions and at the same time preserve the visual and aesthetic unity of the exterior. This plan is what was actually built, and it is essentially what we see today after more than four centuries. El Escorial took almost twenty-five years to build, given all the avatars of personality, technology, politics, and religion.

The building's plan is laid out around an approximately east-west main axis. The basilica is on that axis, designed mainly with single bays, and with well-proportioned extensions that turn the plan into almost a Latin-cross. El Escorial proper is a large rectangle, 740 by 560 Castilian feet (one Castilian foot equals roughly 28 centimeters or 11 inches), the longer sides on the east and west. The basilica is in the center between the shorter north and south sides; and the monastery facilities are in two wings to the south.

One wing forms the main cloister, situated on the southeast quadrant so that the basilica does not shade it; and the other is the monastery proper, formed in a highly geometric fashion around four minor cloisters within the southwest quadrant. These cloisters, or courtyards, are named in the Hieronymite tradition: *de la portería* (entry), *de la hospedería* (hostelry), *de enfermos* (infirmary), and *del cemeterio* (cemetery). For some this arrangement of four squares inside a larger

square distorts the monastery and even destroys it. Others see the pure geometry of Toledo's organized, classicist mind; and still others the influence of Antonio Filarete's Ospedale Maggiore in Milan, especially in this cell along with the symmetrical one on the other side of the east-west axis and the intermediate courtyard between them (now called the Courtyard of the Kings).

With all the stresses of the creative process that led to this plan concentrated in the southern half—the basilica and its front yard—it follows that the northern half of the palace design would have two similar wings. One wing was designed around a large northeast courtyard, symmetrical with the main cloister, and a four-square cell was planned for the northwest quadrant.

Another important consideration was the exact position of the pantheon. The royal burial place, the fountainhead of El Escorial, was to be placed in a basement under the high altar of the basilica. This concentrated it in just ten meters below the basilica's *sancta sanctorum*: the altar and tabernacle, the focal point for all eyes, and the royal burial crypt. No arrangement could be more symbolic, and more architecturally and conceptually logical.

In this way events and circumstances worked to reach the end result. A pantheon called for a monastery, which evolved into a more complex building enveloping a palace, and then a site was selected that allowed a simple but effective geometric, purely rational plan, consonant with the king's personality. This evolution was not that easy, however; it developed from 1559 to 1563. Nonetheless, the basic geometry of the general plan was retained throughout the building process and only a few changes altered the initial scheme.

Two major changes that largely involved the palace area were resolved early in the planning. The first change doubled the monastery capacity from fifty to one hundred monks. This required adding a floor to the four courtyards of the monastery quadrant, forcing for reasons of symmetry the same addition to the palace area in the northwest corner. The second change had a greater impact on the palace: the addition of a college, or seminary, and the enlargement of the library. A small library had been planned for a tower in the center of the south wing, but as the height of the west wing was increased to house the larger community of monks and the college needed a larger library, a connecting tower made no sense (there are still two vertical setoffs where the tower stood). The four courtyards of the northwest quadrant were given to the college, and the library was placed in the main west wing, as a bridge between the monastery and the college.

The part of the palace that remained unaltered, because little alteration was possible in its unique shape and position, was the so-called grill handle. The monastery was dedicated to Saint Lawrence, born in Huesca, in the north of Spain. One of the seven deacons of Pope Sixtus II, the saint was martyred in Rome in A.D. 258 under the Emperor Valerian. As a Roman citizen he was probably beheaded, but the hagiography, after the poet Prudentius and Ambrose, bishop of Milan, represents Saint Lawrence being roasted on a large metal grill. Thus the saint's legendary imagery is associated with the grill and this was the symbol of the monastery. It seems that Dr. Alonso de Almela in the late sixteenth century first suggested that the orthogonal layout of this part of the general plan looked like a grill, with straight-angle axes, courtyards, and wings; the main rectangle represented the grill itself and the wing projecting from the east facade was the grill handle.

This fitted the sixteenth-century mind: the grill, the monastery emblem was repeated over and over again in chalices, dalmatics, architectural drawings, book bindings, and every sort of art object. So simple a symbol was the source of inspiration for artists such as Herrera, Tibaldi, and Titian. Never was a symbol more suitable for a colossal political, religious, and artistic undertaking. This was total coherence of substance and form. The happy connection with the grill also carried a very specific meaning: the battle of Saint Quentin was won by the cavalry of Felipe II's ally, Manuel Filiberto of Savoy, against Constable Montmorency's French army on the feast day of Saint Lawrence, August 10, 1557.

Thus the grill handle of the monastery plan's main east-west axis is the palace of Felipe II and his family. This U-shaped protrusion is built around an open space known as the Mascarons Courtyard, with the ends of the U abutting the end wall of the basilica. The proximity of the royal family to the high altar is obvious, but the two areas are not connected. Looking at the east facade from afar, a svelte, mute stone wall appears. It is the end wall of the basilica with the lower three-story palace attached to it. One side of the palace's ground level opens to a private garden and the other to the Mascarons Courtyard, where the summer rooms are located. The top floor contains the winter rooms, with the service areas on the floor in between. The Mascarons Courtyard measures 13 by 14 meters, a modest size in the huge El Escorial but appropriate for intimate family life.

The palace, though, is far from being rationally arranged for traffic and use. The corridors have granite lintels, a rarity for covering bays, and beam against beam they form a continuous stone ceiling of impressive height leading to the main rooms. The palace has several rooms around the pleasant, relaxing Mascarons Courtyard. One of them is the Promenade Hall, also called the Map Hall (wrongly called the "throne hall," because one is now placed there under a canopy). El Escorial never had a throne. This room, with two windows to the north, two to the south and seven to the east, dominating a broad vista, was originally the Long Gallery, where the king could rest or deal with state affairs as he strolled. The room is in the purest European long-gallery style of the period, as the English scholar John Bury has recently shown. Two long black strips, known as meridian lines, embedded in the ceramic floor of this and the next room indicate with Zodiac signs the sun's reach during each month of the year. These lines are not parallel to the facades, since the building drifts some seventeen degrees relative to the true geographic north.

This large exterior gallery connects with two others that open onto the Mascarons Courtyard, probably used by the king's secretaries. But the actual uses of each of these rooms during the sixteenth century is not certain today; and there were probably changes in purpose and decoration during the first two centuries of the building's existence. It is believed that the bedrooms of the infantes Baltasar Carlos and Felipe Próspero, sons of Felipe IV, were in the Long Gallery in the seventeenth century; but others say this is merely a guess and contend that the princes' rooms were on the lower floor of the north wing, the room now called El Greco Hall. Another room facing north, adjacent to the west stairway of this wing, may have been the guards' room for protecting access to the private area, but this too is an assumption since descriptions of palace life in these earlier periods are brief and not very detailed.

Despite the lack of information about the specific uses of these rooms in the sixteenth and seventeenth centuries, the spirit that animated their architecture remains. The rooms on the upper and lower floors now contain a museum with superb samples of art from the royal collections, including portraits by Pantoja de la Cruz (1553–1608), Claudio Coello (1642–1693), and Juan Carreño de Miranda (1614–1685). These paintings can acquaint us with Carlos I, Manuel Filiberto, or Carlos II. But perhaps the most vivid of all these pictures is the portrait of Felipe II, in his early thirties, handsomely dressed in armor with the Golden Fleece around his neck, painted by the Dutch artist Anton van Dashort Mor, known in Spain as Antonio Moro (1519?–1576).

Another room shows pictures of the royal houses of the time, such as Aranjuez and El Pardo (before its eighteenth-century enlargement by Sabbatini); Campillo; El Bosque in Balsaín; la Casa de las Nieves (the Snow House) in Vaciamadrid; and the overall view of El Escorial. All of the required material for studying the architecture of the Spanish royal palaces is grouped in a single room. The lower floor of this wing is known as the New Museums since their alteration from 1960 to 1965. In it are paintings by Titian, Ribera, Van der Weyden, Sánchez Coello, Tintoretto, and Navarrete, to name only a few. But if only one were to be singled out, this author would choose *The Tunic of Joseph,* painted by Velázquez in 1630 during his first stay in Rome. This painting is a pendant to *The Forge of Vulcan,* now in the Prado Museum. Although neither of these pictures was created as a royal commission, the crown purchased both of them five years later. While the palace has extraordinary works of art, the traditional art center of El Escorial is the basilica and its chapter halls.

When Juan Bautista de Toledo died in 1567, his first assistant, Juan de Herrera (c. 1530–1597) became chief architect of El Escorial. Herrera designed some facades, roofs, and tower spires as well as other areas with such talent that the sober, dignified Escorial style that dominated Spanish architecture for two centuries became known as Herreresque. The exterior design of the building submits to the dictates of the facades in its general layout, materials, and proportions. This makes it impossible to read the palace as such architecturally, since it is integrated into the whole with no singularity or external expression. But this is not true of the inner courtyard facades. The

three facades around what Herrera called the Royal House Courtyard, but popularly is called the Mascarons Courtyard, are notably beautiful, in a classic scheme of three floors each with five openings. The ground floor has half-round arches above the columns; those of the north and south fronts were closed later, unfortunately with mock-stone parapets. On the west side, two fountains spout water from the mascarons, hence the courtyard's name. The fountains were intended to delight the royal family with their sound and to water the flowerbeds and plants that embellished this restful area.

The openings on the second story are balconies and those on the top floor are windows, some open and some blind, ornamented with soft moldings to promote, along with the water and flowers, feelings of peace, elegance, and intimacy. This U-shaped wing is what Fernando Chueca has accurately called "the private palace," as opposed to two other small wings, symmetrical and separated from one another. These last two are "the intimate palace," the lodgings of the king and queen. A mere cluster of five rooms each, they are the epitome of royal privacy, where the king worked, relaxed, and prayed. Each apartment is barely one hundred meters square.

The king's rooms include a soberly decorated general purpose hall of 5 by 10 meters with clay floor tiles, Talavera glazed tile wainscot, whitewashed walls up to the vaulted ceiling. Gray marble frames the hall's openings: two windows that look out to the private garden, another to the east, an entry door, and a door leading to two other rooms. The larger room was the bedroom and the smaller one the office, with a desk. Two more rooms completed the assembly, virtually hollowed out from the four-meter thick wall that encloses the high-altar space. These two rooms are small oratories, each only three meters square, finely bedecked in marble and jasper, connecting the bedroom and office with the high altar, which is treated with the same materials. This is an intentional decorative change from the severe ceramic flooring and whitewashed walls of the king's private rooms.

The union of God and king becomes total. Philip II could follow the Holy Services from his bed when he was resting or ill, or from his office when he was working. No monarchy by Divine Right has been more aware of the source of its power, and none so materialized this awareness through architecture. With this space and functional layout, Felipe II was constantly close to his God, and below was the sculpture of himself at prayer, with his son and his wives who were already dead when Pompeo Leoni was commissioned to do this group. The king was above the pantheon that held his father's remains and that would eventually hold his own. In the background was the cenotaph of his aunts, the queens María and Leonor. It would seem impossible to achieve a greater coherence and clarity of ideas, a more faithful architectural expression of political and religious concepts.

Felipe II was able to create a personal cosmos in just one hundred square meters. There were pictures by Hieronymus Bosch (c. 1450–1516), one of his favorite painters, religious panel paintings, and portraits of his parents, Carlos V and Isabel, to link sacred, worldly, and family life. These rooms may not have been as austere as we see them today; their nakedness may have been softened with carpets and cordovan leather. Nonetheless, they did not meet the same demands for comfort of Renaissance or modern patrons.

At the opposite side of the high altar, symmetrical with the king's apartment, is a similar apartment for the queen. But which queen? She was not the French Isabel de Valois, who married Felipe II in 1560 and died in 1568, when work at the El Escorial was only in its first five years. Isabel gave Felipe two daughters, Isabel Clara Eugenia and Catalina Micaela, and her death so saddened the king that it is said that even his personality changed.

In 1570 the king married his fourth wife, his niece Ana de Austria, who died in 1580 when the royal lodgings were still not ready. The Infanta Isabel Clara Eugenia was the royal person who actually lived in the queen's quarters, and she gave her name to the apartment. These rooms contain two fine portraits of those beloved daughters of the king. There was also a portrait of Felipe II in which Sánchez Coello depicted the king's deep, intense eyes, but the painting disappeared in the mid-1980s.

The private lodgings were to have two back towers flanking the high altar to balance the volume of the two front towers, but the back towers were never built. In keeping with an old Spanish, and universal, tradition, the king's quarters are oriented to the south, and the queen's to the north. This tradition was respected in the royal lodgings of Aranjuez but inexplicably not in Balsaín's Casa del Bosque.

The private palace, or grill handle, and the apartments of the king and queen looked on secluded gardens well defined by granite walls and a rectangular geometry; they had sand floors and boxwood plantings. These gardens can be seen now from the Canapés Room, because some of the surrounding walls were lowered to comply with a decree enacted in the nineteenth century by the liberal government of Isabel II. The southeast wall corner was also lowered to allow a view of the monastery pond. The king's private garden and the friars' garden and pond had been hidden from public view for almost three hundred years.

A summary timetable of the palace itself within the large El Escorial complex may be useful. It was begun in 1570, once the vaults reaching the ground level were closed in that area. In 1572 this level was also closed in the areas near the basilica. The north wing, the boundary of the palace, was in process the following year. The pace picked up somewhat in 1575 when Juan de Herrera's growing influence ordered the building stones shaped at the quarry instead of on the site as was done previously. This simplified the work since the stonemasons then had to make only minor adjustments to fit the pieces. An unknown master left the best testimony of the state of the construction in 1576, an eloquent aerial-view drawing of the north facade. It seems that one such drawing was made for each facade, but the other three are lost.

The two southern quadrants, constituting the monastery, were basically finished at that time as well as the grill handle and the bases of the two towers that were never built. The drawing shows intense work underway on the basilica, where more than ten of the large cranes designed by Herrera were busy erecting its walls and the four large piers of the transept. The two northern quadrants, that is, the college and the northeast part of the palace, were considerably behind, as only the perimeter walls were built, up to the cornice. It matters little who did this rendering—known as the Hatfield House Drawing because it is owned by Lord Salisbury. The artist could be a Fleming, or Fabrizio Castello, or Francisco de Holanda, or Herrera himself, as has been suggested. What matters is that we know that the northeast and southeast quadrants, including the college and the library, were relatively delayed.

The contract for the Mascarons Courtyard and the Herrera-designed private palace was awarded in 1578 and the contract for the fountains and niches of this courtyard in 1579. In 1581 the erection of the northern facades and bays progressed rapidly. But two years earlier it was already known that the palace was too small and had to grow. The space restrictions imposed on the northeast quadrant by the college forced the invasion of the large courtyard by a T-shaped addition only thirty feet high (half that of the wings around it) to the public palace. The addition's original layout is little known since no substantial set of drawings exists. We know that the west side was dedicated to the queen, with direct access to her rooms, but this is modified today. The kitchens were on the west side of the main block, as a sign left on the walls indicates: *"cozina de boca de sus magestades"* (kitchen for Their Majesties' mouths). At present, visitors enter through one of the kitchens, which has two post-and-lintel recesses with large fireplaces in the floor and at the top of its opposite wall direct exhausts for smoke.

A double-bay north wing was known as the Sala de los Caballeros (Gentlemen's Hall). The ground floor had a lobby, a guard room, and dining rooms by the kitchens. To the left, the east side of this wing, were the Ambassadors Hall and an open service stairway as well as other ancillary stairways and facilities. There is, finally, a large, oblong Private Royal Gallery in the upper floor, 60 by 6 meters, separated from the basilica by a blind wall; and another opposite this, with nine windows looking over the courtyards and galleries of the private palace. This gallery is the much publicized Battle Hall, because of the scenes of medieval wars and others fought by Felipe II against France and Portugal. Again, John Bury may be right in suggesting that this was another long gallery used by the king to stroll unseen and watch his agents, secretaries, and ambassadors entering the palace.

The palace size was reduced, first by the college and then by the enlarged monastery, and it had to grow outward, beyond the original plan. The Casa de los Doctores was begun in 1583, but in 1581, the first Casa de Oficios had been started, with the second in 1587. These were two buildings paralleling the north facade to house the *"mouth services"* (personal royal services) required by the Burgundian etiquette of the Spanish court, services that could not be accommodated in the palace proper.

Each day in the life of Felipe II and his retinue required an enormous array of servants, baggage, horses, and services. Herrera's talent was put to the test again when he had to complete simultaneously the monastery and these two separate buildings, which harmonize so well with the north facade of the palace. Both houses, plus the Grimaldi Passageway between them, measure 156,8 meters, exactly the length of the north facade of El Escorial and their cornices too are the same height. This side of the esplanade constitutes a well-balanced urban space. The absence of towers, ornamentation, and axes shows that these buildings are intended to serve the palace. The back facades of the two buildings have one story less than the front ones to overcome the difference in level between the esplanade and the present Floridablanca street, called Doctors' street in the sixteenth and seventeenth centuries because a house of the same name was located slightly to the west on that street. The stables required by the palace and the Casas de Oficios were situated on the other side of that street.

The imprecisions of this outline stem from insufficient information concerning the arrangement of the intimate, family, and public spaces within El Escorial, where four Spanish kings of the Hapsburg dynasty lived, Felipe II, Felipe III, Felipe IV, and Carlos II, from 1585 to 1700. Dynastic change brought a lessened use of El Escorial, because the newer palaces in La Granja and Madrid, built by the new king, Felipe V, were dedicated to the greater glory of the Bourbon dynasty. Felipe V's successor, Fernando VI, similarly devoted efforts and money to a new structure, building a church in Madrid, the Salesas, where he and his wife, Bárbara, are buried.

The true transformation of El Escorial was profound. It took place in the late eighteenth century under Carlos III and Carlos IV, and was finished by Fernando VII. The transformation was now total: It affected the interior layout, the functional arrangement, the decor, and part of the north wing. Some critics find this reconstruction useless, overdone, and avoidable, since with a little restoration almost the same results could have been achieved. They are probably right, but two centuries later this criticism is meaningless. The modifications were entrusted to the talented architect Juan de Villanueva

(1739–1811), the best architect in eighteenth-century Spain. Villanueva obtained his degree in 1767 after a long apprenticeship in Rome with a grant from the Real Academia de Bellas Artes, and he received his first commissions to enlarge El Escorial from Carlos III. The new House of Infantes followed the same enlargement plan Herrera used two centuries earlier in the Casas de Oficios, but this time facing the west facade of the monastery. Villanueva's building has a well-composed facade with a long stone dado. The new building is extraordinarily respectful of the overall design of El Escorial. A third Casa de Oficios was added on the north to form an L-shaped esplanade, completing the proportioned and homogeneous urban plan that Herrera began in such a masterful way. This esplanade framed El Escorial with a unity of materials and concepts that only a genius like Villanueva could have achieved. Only he could have dared to design new buildings around El Escorial.

Two highly interesting buildings, also by Villanueva, belong to the "external palace" of El Escorial, the pavilions named the Casita de Abajo and Casita de Arriba (The Little House Below and The Little House Above). The first, also called the Casita del Príncipe (The Prince's Little House), is a very delicate and prettily furnished house, surrounded by gardens and inspired by English models to which Villanueva could refer in his library. The Casita del Príncipe was built in two distinct stages for the Prince of Asturias and future King Carlos IV, on lower ground than El Escorial and near the town. Its granite, pargeting, and slate echo El Escorial, blended with eighteenth-century touches. Its interior decoration has remained almost intact and it is a building that must be visited.

The Casita de Arriba, also excellent, fine, and compact architecturally, was built for the infante Don Gabriel, Carlos IV's brother and son of Carlos III. The infante married a Portuguese infanta, died a widower in 1788 at the age of thirty-eight, and thus enjoyed his little pavilion for only ten years. The marvelous view of El Escorial from this location was carefully chosen. An alteration made by the mid-twentieth century changed it slightly, but the central hall around which the building was designed is still an eighteenth-century music room with oculi on the upper level where the orchestra played. Young Prince Juan Carlos lived in this house for some months.

But Villanueva's most important work was within El Escorial itself. In 1788, after the death of Carlos III, his son Carlos IV ordered a substantial change of the royal lodgings in the northeast corner that not only affected the floor plan but also the original north facade. Modern critics reproach the royal decision to alter the palace, not only because it was hardly justified but because it caused the demise of the public palace designed for Felipe II.

This criticism is justified in that the entire north wing had to be altered to force a carriage entrance to what is now called the carriage courtyard, in what some consider a bold alteration of the Founding Charter of the Monastery that provided this rule of entry: "No animals or beasts, only men of reason." Probably Carlos IV was not aware of it, or maybe he simply reasoned that after all Felipe II had been dead for two centuries, because he wanted to enter the palace in his coach. From the coach entrance, a new stairway linked the new carriage courtyard with the royal lodgings on the main floor. To do this, the main door had to be moved six meters to the east, forcing the college door to be moved to the west in order to maintain the symmetry. Still visible are two stone scars that record the demand for entering the palace without descending from a carriage.

The critics are also right in saying that the new stairway is so crowded into the space and lacking in proportion and majesty that Villanueva himself surely could not have thought it was a good job. He had designed much better stairways fifteen or twenty years earlier for the House of the Infantes. One has to think that the new stairway was a royal imposition to satisfy a whim. But this criticism is rather pointless, because if an austere, retrained palace was lost, a new Bourbon palace was gained, shining with the tapestries, color, and gilt that were much to the taste of the eighteenth century. At least the decorative changes were highly coherent in style, and the mark of the Enlightenment in literature, theater and music was also shown in the lively, well-lighted rooms of Carlos IV and María Luisa. A brilliant palace with gold, red, and blue silks and new carpets from the Royal Tapestry Workshop replaced the cordovans, old monochrome carpets, and almost monastic woodwork of the old palace.

The lodgings of Carlos IV, in the northeast, or Damas tower, are not shown to the public, because the furniture is highly fragile. This furniture, however, is of the finest woods and it illustrates the pure luxury of the Spanish royal quarters. These quarters—the office, oratory, toilet, and receiving rooms—constitute a new decorative *sancta sanctorum* in El Escorial.

If the sixteenth-century palace was an emporium of paintings, the new palace was a treasury of tapestries. One name stands out among their designers: Francisco Goya (1746–1828). Goya's presence in the new porcelain room, dining room, antechambers, audience hall, and so many others, makes Maella, Bayeu, even Téniers and Houasse, seem pale. Young Goya, designer to the Royal Tapestry Workshop, infuriated the weavers with his glazes, his chiaroscuro, his new tonalities, and his audacity of color and subject. These are seen throughout a tour of the palace. At the end of the tour is the Third Queen's Hall, filled with tapestries depicting late eighteenth-century life. Then, through a small door, one enters the Battle Hall and in just two steps moves back two centuries, from Carlos IV to Felipe II, from the Enlightenment to the Counterreformation.

El Escorial palace, intermittently from its foundation to the early twentieth century, was a royal family residence, where kings and infantes were born, lived, and died; and for three centuries it was a center of political power. The royal family stayed there in the autumn and also during Holy Week to attend Masses. Felipe II died in El Escorial, and Fernando VII, the controversial king at the time of the Napoleonic invasion and the first constitution, was born in El Escorial. Bloody events had taken place there earlier, in the time of Carlos II and his favorite Juan José de Austria, and shortly thereafter during the War of Spanish Succession.

Queen Isabel II and her daughters Paz and Eulalia stayed at El Escorial in 1878, when the banished queen came out of exile in Paris to organize the wedding of her son Alfonso XII, since the government forbade her to reside in the Royal Palace in Madrid.

One of the last alterations in the palace was made about 1925, to recondition the east wing for the dictator General Primo de Rivera. This was the last time the palace was a residence, for a leader if not for a king.

Now El Escorial itself is a museum piece, though only part of it is shown to the public. Occasionally it is used for official functions, and in it the echoes of Herrera, Titian, Velázquez, Goya, Felipe II, and Carlos IV can still be heard.

The PALACE of ARANJUEZ

The PALACE of ARANJUEZ

✛

All Spanish royal palaces have reciprocal relationships with their environments. Thus the Royal Palace in Madrid has shaped sections of the city near the palace. La Granja converted wild nature into beautiful gardens and created a surrounding town. This happened too at El Pardo and La Almudaina, the latter the original cell of the concentric urban development of Palma de Mallorca. Riofrío is the exception. Located in a marvelous, hardly transformed landscape, the palace was never completed, and it has been inhabited only briefly in its 250 years of life.

This palace-environment relationship is particularly strong in Aranjuez. In the often quoted words of an ancient historian: "Aranjuez is a gift of the Tagus." The origin and evolution of this palace is intimately tied to the Tagus River, which meanders through a broad valley. On the north bank, the river is flanked by the almost vertical cliffs of Seseña and the selenious hills of Añover; and on the south by the gentler hummocks in Ontígola, Ocaña, and Yepes.

The Tagus runs south from its source, skirts the Alcarria and turns sharply west toward the wide valley, where it is fed by the Jarama. Aranjuez is precisely at the confluence with the Jarama. Its origin is uncertain. Some writers place it at the end of the eleventh century, when the Christian kingdom of Castilla reached the Tagus and took Toledo. Others believe Aranjuez originated later, after Alfonso VIII won the battle of Las Navas in 1212 and gave the land to the Knights of Santiago. About 1387 Suárez de Figueroa, the Order's grand master, built a palace as a central location for its possessions in the surrounding area. Although the religious center of the Order was in Uclés, there was no better place for a recreation house than this well-watered, fertile valley with its generous supply of game for the nobility and the leading Knights of the Order.

Aranjuez is built on a wide S-shaped meander. A natural wall in the first curve creates a low dam that diverts part of the flow to a small channel in a westerly direction, while the main river turns to the north. The master house was built in the first curve of the S in the fourteenth century, and some of its walls remained until the beginning of the eighteenth century. Nine hundred meters downstream, channel and river come together again, and the island that is formed gives its name to the garden, La Isla. Many contend that this dam, improved by Juan Bautista de Toledo, the first architect of El Escorial, is not only the historical origin of the palace but also the source of its name, as it was called Aranzuel or Aranzueje (probably "wooded valley" in old Basque).

In the fifteenth century, this pleasant site with the master house became the property of the crown, then the united crowns of Castilla and Aragón. Isabel and Fernando were ready to give Spain a new state in accordance with modern times. Two powerful medieval institutions—the nobility and the orders of knighthood—would submit to the power of a monarchy. In 1476 the grand master of the Knights of Santiago, Rodrigo Manrique, died in Ocaña, near Aranjuez. He was mourned by his son Jorge Manrique in one of the most beautiful poems in Spanish literature. Queen Isabel had no qualms about appearing at the order's chapter meeting for the election of a new master to force the choice of her own candidate. The royal will of Isabel and Fernando was clear. In 1490 they obtained a bull from Pope Innocent VIII granting the crown the right to rule the knighthood orders as the offices of grand master became vacated. The Order of Calatrava was incorporated by the Crown that same year, that of Santiago in 1493, and Alcántara in 1494. The Order of Montesa was not taken over until 1587. Thus the Aranjuez master house became a royal house, frequently visited by the king and queen. A new papal provision from Adrian VI in 1523 affirmed the perpetual incorporation of the grand masterships to Carlos I and his successors.

No plans exist of the master house, but from written descriptions we know it was a square Mudéjar-style building with a central courtyard; a statue of Carlos I is believed to have stood in its center until the mid-sixteenth century. Some ancillary buildings were probably near the main house. The property also had well-irrigated land, tree-lined paths, wooded areas full of game that were carefully kept by imperial order, and the garden of La Isla. The Hapsburgs were intent on improving what was called the Heredamiento (inheritance) of the Aranjuez area, anticipating its exploitation by the kings of the Enlightenment period two centuries later.

We know that as a child Felipe II (1527–1598) lived for long periods in Aranjuez. He was already a lover of nature, and his tutor Juan de Zúñiga informed the emperor Carlos V of the boy's enthusiasm for outdoor activity. At thirteen, Felipe asked permission to go into the woods to try his crossbow, and "he rode his horse in the forest for six hours, which to him seemed like two." His personal interest in Aranjuez led naturally to a building commitment, since he already had in mind the paternalistic idea of converting the privileged site into a large complex comprised of an elegant villa surrounded by gardens, large tree-lined promenades, and a hydraulic system of dams and canals to facilitate travel and irrigation. Palace, gardens, and promenades became a reality through the years but not the canals. Both Carlos and Felipe had seen Europe criss-crossed by fluvial ways, and they tried to make the Tagus navigable from Aranjuez to Toledo, in a first phase, and then from there to Lisbon. Carlos had considered linking the Ebro at its source with the Bay of Biscay, so it is not strange that the Tagus suggested a network of canals. Only some minor watering ditches were built, but the villa itself was completed.

His mind set on the Aranjuez residence, the prince commissioned his architect Juan Bautista de Toledo (d. 1567) to design it. Felipe's idea was not a symbolic palace, and not even an alcazar, but rather a country villa on the site of the old house of the Knights of Santiago. Juan Bautista's solution was in keeping with the site and the king's wish: a house open to nature with clear views of the countryside but with secluded areas as well. The scheme for Aranjuez was not a closed alcazar like El Pardo or a complex layout like the one the architect was designing for El Escorial, nor was it to follow the model of the Casa del Bosque in Balsaín, although its function was similar. The novel and unexpected feature of the new house was its coexistence with the old one. In other words, the house designed by Toledo and begun about 1564, stood together with the older structures until about 1715.

The new villa was to be built on top of the old house by the curve in the river where the channel departs from the main course, its four sides similarly oriented to the four cardinal points. But it took a century and a half to complete. Only the southern half was built, the wing that Spanish tradition reserves for the king's quarters. The new plan was an elongated rectangle 120 by 20 meters with its longer facade looking west; its east end connected to a smaller wing 60 by 45 meters; and its central courtyard was approximately where the old house's courtyard had been. The chapel, situated at the south end of the longer wing, was curiously high and square, 11 by 11 meters in plan, with a large stairway cube attached to it for all services except the king's.

Because of the poor condition of the south side of the medieval house, it was determined that the construction of the new one should begin on that side. We know the chapel was built first, then the longer wing, more or less up to the middle of its planned length, followed by the south side of the U connected to the east. The work was carried out simultaneously with other building projects, such as El Pardo and El Escorial, that required large sums of money, and consequently its pace was rather slow. In 1567 Toledo died unexpectedly, at the time he was building a wooden model of Aranjuez. The project was temporarily entrusted to the master builder Jerónimo Gili until the appointment of Juan de Herrera (c. 1530–1597), the architect of El Escorial.

Drawings in the Vatican Library, made by the royal architect Juan Gómez de Mora almost sixty years later, throw considerable light on Toledo's design. Toledo had projected the south side for the king's rooms, the north for the queen's, and the east for an assortment of other rooms. The west, the longest side, had two projecting wings for the main access hallway with lateral stairways leading to the chapel in the south end and to the theater in the north end; the central section was reserved for reception halls. These plans are very revealing because the areas built until 1626 are shown in yellow. These areas amount to a little less than the southern half corresponding to the king's quarters. As for the rest of the building in the drawing, Gómez de Mora's manuscript mentions a number of foundations that could not yet be completed.

Research published by Professor Javier Rivera of the University of Valladolid, an expert on Juan Bautista de Toledo, affirms that Toledo was the author of the entire Aranjuez design. He planned an east-west axis of symmetry with two royal quarters, for the king and the queen, each with an adjacent private garden enclosed by walls. These walls were thick enough to permit strolling in order to look at the gardens from above, recalling the Balsaín house. The attribution to Toledo seems justified, since features in the villa of Aranjuez relate it to the private palace of El Escorial formed around the Mascarons Courtyard. Furthermore, it seems illogical that Felipe II would have agreed to an open plan that allowed the palace to grow by whimsical, unplanned additions, much less from an architect who took almost two years to produce a general plan for El Escorial, his main commission.

Herrera included the full layout of the palace in his drawings of 1581 for the Picotajo vegetable gardens in the Aranjuez area. No doubt he included the layout after the plans of his teacher as a sign of respect and with the certainty that Toledo's overall scheme would eventually be built.

It was possible to follow the chapel services in the royal quarters from either the ground or the main floor. The king's lodgings on the main floor looked south into his private garden, which was a marvel of color and delight within a rectangle of 25 by 45 meters. The ground floor was an arcade open to this garden, and the king's quarters were articulated around two main stairways, one next to the chapel and the other for his own use. The location, shape, and functions of the stairways cause some confusion in respect to Toledo's overall plans, particularly since there is no absolute symmetry in the later drawing by Gómez de Mora. In fact, the queen's stairway, symmetrical with the king's, was never built, nor was the north side of her

garden closed. Not even the width of the north wing—21 meters—is the same as that of the south—17 meters. But the lack of symmetry generally responds to well-justified functional requirements.

More difficult to support is the theory in fashion until quite recently that Aranjuez was designed as an asymmetrical villa, dominated by the chapel spire and consisting only of what was built in the sixteenth century, that is, an L-shaped building enveloping the king's garden. A general plan with double services, stairways, and gardens for the king and the queen is more believable. Two south halls were recently uncovered on the ground floor of the long wing, which show Toledo and Herrera's ideas on layout, treatment, and materials. The external hall looking west was open with a portico. The palace facade was a happy mixture of white limestone quarried in nearby Colmenar de Oreja and reddish brick "fired in the Flemish manner" at Felipe II's personal request. A simple decorative element was added to the classic Tuscan pilasters and half-round arches: rectangular limestone panels placed on the rich brickwork background over the main lintels. Toledo did the same thing on the facade of the Convent of the Descalzas Reales in Madrid (1564–1567). The Aranjuez lodgings, supported by the old master house and service buildings, were reserved for royal visits in spring, the season when the many colors and aromas of the gardens are at their best. Felipe II, Felipe III, Felipe IV, and Carlos II used these buildings for more than a century.

An attempt by Felipe IV to finish the house in 1636 never went beyond some preliminary drawings by his architect Juan Gómez de Mora (1586–1647), who planned a substantial change in Toledo's scheme. Gómez de Mora introduced a large imperial stairway in the main vestibule at the center of the long wing, instead of the two separate stairways for the king and the queen. But the 12-meter bay needed to accommodate a stairway of this size meant a projection that would break the main facade. This design that was never executed is interesting in that it anticipated the ideas and symbols of the Bourbon dynasty that were so successfully carried out a century later.

Aranjuez, under Felipe IV, witnessed more festive occasions than under his father, Felipe III, whose character was sanctimonious, aloof, and little inclined to worldly pleasures. After Felipe III died in 1621 everything changed. In spring of that year, after the official mourning period ended, the new king was hailed with fireworks. Tournaments and masquerades were the amusements preferred by the court. The festivities held at Aranjuez in spring 1622 are famous. Plays by Villamediana, Mendoza, and Lope de Vega were performed; *La Gloria de Niquea* was the most notable. The private garden of Felipe II also was improved. Felipe IV renewed the old pavements and placed medallions of Emperor Carlos V and Empress Isabel on the facade along with an excellent marble statue by Pompeo Leoni (c. 1533–1608) of Felipe II. Parties were also given in Aranjuez in honor of the ill-fated Prince of Wales, Charles, who was in Madrid to arrange his marriage with Felipe IV's daughter, the Infanta María.

The Palace of Aranjuez was occasionally plundered to decorate other palaces, for example, the statues that were moved to the Buen Retiro in 1634. Yet Aranjuez was never devoid of fine works of art, and the royal family were very contented there. As a result of the fire in the Buen Retiro on February 29, 1640, the spring season in Aranjuez had to begin earlier than usual. Prince Baltasar Carlos, only eleven years old, asked his father's proud minister—the Count-Duke of Olivares, creator of the Buen Retiro palace as a gift to the king—why he had never been taken to Aranjuez before. Just one of the Aranjuez gardens, the prince remarked, was worth more than the entire Buen Retiro.

The yearly trips to El Escorial, El Pardo, and Aranjuez were so costly that they had to be prudently administered. One month in Aranjuez cost twice as much as a month in El Buen Retiro and one-and-a-half times more than a month in El Escorial. Professor Domínguez Ortiz, a specialist in seventeenth-century Spanish history, points out that those journeys were so costly because of an erroneous concept of majesty. They required a formidable train of dozens of vehicles, beasts of burden, and servants that could progress only four or five leagues a day, like a slow and exorbitant cloud of locusts. The last trip Felipe IV made, to Pheasants Island (on the Spanish-French border) to deliver his daughter to the French delegation and arrange her wedding to Louis XIV, cost one million ducats, an astronomic sum that could damage the wealthiest public treasury.

There is little information on new construction at Aranjuez during the second half of the seventeenth century, nor was the palace significantly modified until the early eighteenth century. The building activity of Felipe V is usually explained by his freedom to devote himself to improving the royal palaces after the War of Succession in 1714. Although this is true, wars continued during his reign. There were other reasons, especially the large amounts of energy brought to bear by the king's second wife, Isabel de Farnesio (Isabella Farnese). Another key to building expansion and new construction was that a new dynasty needs a new image. Aranjuez could not remain half-built.

In 1715 Felipe V commissioned architect Pedro Caro Idrogo (d. 1732) to resume the Aranjuez project, a job that occupied him for more than fifteen years. Caro completed the main square but without strictly following Gómez de Mora or Toledo's designs. He built a new north wing next to the river curve with a layout that was not symmetrical to the south wing, breaking the tradition of parity between the lodgings of the king and the queen. With no explanation, he also altered the proportions of the new wing by making it three meters wider than the north wing. This can only be observed by looking at the drawings of the floor plans. Another change that has not been well explained and is more noticeable is that the north facade departed from the style of the south facade, and above all from the overly bare east facade, which was supposed to open onto the gardens to receive morning sunshine.

But Caro's major innovation, at least on paper, was to do away with the vestibules in the center of both the ground and the main floors of the west facade and install in their place an ambitiously designed, rounded double stairway. This beautiful concept, a novelty in its time, was never built. The always well-informed José Luis Sancho explains that the destructive interference of Juan Antonio Samaniego, the governor of the royal site may explain this. Caro's elegant drawings are full of Samaniego's notes, or rather his corrections. There is hardly a room or a facade that he does not revise. Not even Scotti dared go that far with Sacchetti's designs for the palace in Madrid, or with Rabaglio's for Riofrío.

Seeing Caro's plans, more than corrected, blemished by Samaniego makes one feel sorry for Caro, who managed to complete the main body of the palace against such odds, even though in an extremely simplified form. With such an inquisitor, architecture could not be created freely. Caro died in 1732 and was followed by Etienne Marchand, who in turn died one year later and was replaced by Léandre Bachelieu.

The participation of other masters during the so-called Caro Idrogo period is recorded. Among them were Teodoro Ardemans and Juan Román, who worked almost concurrently on the design and construction of La Granja. But the main figure in this first half of the eighteenth century (aside from Filippo Juvarra's brief involvement in very specific matters, such as the garden facade cornices) was a painter-decorator-architect who worked in the theatrical style used in Baroque palaces: Giacomo Bonavia (1705–1759). Bonavia had been working in Spain for seven years when he was commissioned in 1735 to resolve the problem of the main stairway, that majestic stairway filling the vestibule first conceived by Gómez de Mora and still unbuilt in Caro's time. Bonavia worked for ten years in Aranjuez, and his masterpiece is the magnificent vestibule stairway that Juan Bautista Toledo designed 180 years earlier. Bonavia's plan was a space 23-meters wide in which the stairway occupied 15 meters. Thus a corridor 4-meters wide at either side reached the center courtyard. On the outside this solution yielded three doors. Tradition reserved the center door for removing the king's body should he die in the palace, while the side doors were used for everyday royal entrances and exits. The carriage stopped in the corridor by the stairway and the king descended; the carriage then went on to the central courtyard, turned around, and exited by the other door. So Bonavia's sense of drama did not lack functionality. The center door was never opened, because no king died at Aranjuez. Queen Mother Isabel de Farnesio died there, and as tradition required she was removed by the side door.

Felipe V began the transformation of Aranjuez and his son Fernando VI continued it, but the monarch who really changed the image and size of the palace was Carlos III (1716–1788). He was not short of stamina, although he came back to Spain already a mature man. It is said of this very capable king that his true ability was in choosing highly competent collaborators. Carlos had complete confidence in Francesco Sabbatini (1722–1797), an ambitious engineer and architect born in Palermo, a man with extraordinary entrepreneurial and artistic abilities. Sabbatini doubled the size of the palace of

El Pardo, designed a formidable extension for Madrid's Royal Palace, although only a small part was executed, and conceived two wings for Aranjuez, one that emerged from the old theater and the other from the chapel.

These new wings together with the old main facade formed a parade ground, or honor courtyard, in the established growth pattern of the old alcazars. The two-story wings measure 90 by 12 meters each, which added some 7,000 square meters to the palace, almost doubling its size. In this way Sabbatini met the royal requirement to make room for the king's sizeable family. Enlargement projects usually have aesthetic costs, but Sabbatini adapted his design notably well to the previous style, maintaining the modules, materials, colors, and proportions so that the whole building would look as if it were designed and made by the same hand, and so it seems.

The new wings are highly rational. Each has three bays, a narrow one facing north to serve as a corridor, an interior bay for services, and a wider exterior bay facing south. Sabbatini placed the party hall at the end of the north wing and the chapel at the end of the south wing. Both are first class. The party hall, 22 by 12 meters with five windows, has splendid proportions, but the vault painting that Anton Raphael Mengs (1728–1779) left unfinished is the most outstanding element. The stages of his work are clearly shown: the charcoal preliminary drawing, contours, tonal scheme, backgrounds, and the impastoes and even the final details in some sections. The chapel is equally successful, a happy mixture of a *pianta centrale* and an elongated 20-meter nave, with well-solved traffic patterns and paired linear and helicoid stairs. Two magnificent vault frescoes by Francisco Bayeu (1734–1795) complete the excellent work by Sabbatini. The architect also projected a long balcony with five openings from the center of each wing on the courtyard side.

Sabbatini's enlargement enriched the town's westerly growth by interposing a large plaza with rounded ends, Raso de la Estrella (Esplanade of the Star). The so-called Bourbon trident of tree-lined avenues sprang from this plaza. Under Fernando VI, Aranjuez grew in the Dutch manner, as the Romantics termed it later. As a result, the old Casas de Oficios designed by Herrera now faced the ample plaza of San Antonio in a north-south direction, with the chapel of the same name at the far end. In this way, when Bourbon energy forced the royal site of Aranjuez to grow in the mid-eighteenth century, two major axes, the palace (east-west) and the new plaza (north-south), articulated the site's model development. In a few years the town had adapted to late Baroque aesthetics and city-planning tendencies.

But researcher José Luis Sancho has pointed out that many traces of the seventeenth century were lost. The spirit that exudes from the celebrated, anonymous view of Aranjuez was retained in El Escorial but has been practically lost here. Sabbatini broke up the chapel and theater fronts with new walls, and he shaved off the pilasters on the west facade to fit the new wings. Thus Felipe II's perfume evaporated forever. The two wings were built rapidly, from 1771 to 1774. Since then, Aranjuez has had two approaches, the traditional one from the east and a new one through the no longer extant Green Bridge, which permitted access by way of the trident, looking toward the old east facade framed by the two wings added by Carlos III.

In the nineteenth century Aranjuez continued to be a center of political power, and a few significant interior additions were made. A very celebrated one is the smoking room designed by Rafael Contreras (1824–1890) in Moorish style, a style he understood well. But the main halls have been virtually untouched in the last two centuries.

Aside from its architecture, the palace of Aranjuez contains many fine works of art. It would be difficult to point out the best from such an excellent collection, but the superb white marble bust of Louis XIV by Antoine Coysevox (1640–1720), the frescoes by Mariano Maella (1739–1819) and Francisco Bayeu (1734–1795), and the *Christ* of Anton Raphael Mengs (1728–1779) deserve mention. According to Jonathan Brown, another painting stands out, the *Orpheus Charming the Animals* by the prolific Neapolitan painter Lucca Giordano (1632–1705). The other great artist represented in Aranjuez is Corrado Giaquinto (1700–1765), chamber painter to Fernando VI from 1752. Although most of Giaquinto's work in Spain is associated with the Royal Palace of Madrid, his painting in the State Dining Room of Aranjuez is formidable. Once the sitting room of the prince of Asturias (later king Carlos IV), this is fortunately one of the rooms where the eighteenth-century spirit is wholly preserved. The vault is by Giacomo Amigoni (c. 1685–1752), who also painted the round motifs in the door transoms. But no doubt his best pieces are the Life of Joseph scenes: *Joseph in Jail, Presentation of Jacob to the Pharaoh, The Drinking Glass in Benjamin's Bag,* and *The Triumph of Joseph,* all originally designed for tapestries. Among the three other works in this room by Giaquinto, *Children's Games* is a true Rococo masterpiece. Giaquinto left the Spanish court in 1762, no doubt because of the arrival of Anton Raphael Mengs, a cold academician, heir to the Carraccis' classicism and Carlos III's preferred taste. The Porcelain Room, designed by Bonavia and his teacher Galluzzi, is another fine, elegant room. Construction began in the time of Felipe V, but only the marble floor was completed then. The porcelain panels that cover the walls and ceiling were made at the Buen Retiro Royal China Workshop, which was already under Carlos III.

The brilliant late eighteenth-century years of the Bourbon dynasty produced La Casita del Labrador (Farmer's Little House), or simply La Casita, in the heart of the Prince's Garden. Never was a prince more beloved than the good Carlos, and never was a king more loathed by a disappointed populace than Carlos IV. La Casita was built over a period of ten years without a master plan, and its decoration is much better than its architecture. The first stage was built in 1790, a rectangular building clearly in the style of Juan de Villanueva, who added two wings during 1799–1800. Along with the first structure this formed a small honor courtyard with lateral arcades and terraces. The decorator of these wings was the Frenchman Jean-Demosthène Dugourc. The third phase, the ornamentation of the facades, was attributed to Isidoro González Velázquez. The rich and creative interior, which is perfectly preserved condition, surprises the visitor because of the sharp contrast between the building and its contents. One is undecided about where to go first—the Sculpture Gallery, the Billiard Room, the Ballroom, or the Saleta. But the Platinum Room may be the most bewildering to visitors. The decor is a tribute to its authors, who knew how to work within a unified plan. Fabrics, carpets, vases, lamps, clocks, marbles, furniture, and stuccos are perfectly attuned to each other as if directed by an orchestra conductor. Few Spanish palace decorations have successfully withstood so many changes and events as the Casita in Aranjuez.

The bucolic and artistic life of Aranjuez began to tremble in

1808 under the threat posed by Napoleon. Carlos IV and his minister Manuel Godoy were nominally allies of the emperor and the French troops arrived as friends, but fearing that they would change their attitude in the face of the enmity of the Spanish people, the king and his favorite planned to move the court to Cádiz, and if necessary to Spanish America. There was no time. On March 18, 1808, a mutiny broke out in Aranjuez. Godoy was taken prisoner near the palace and Carlos IV was forced to abdicate to his son Fernando. The power vacuum created by the forced exile of the royal family in France was filled by spontaneously organized provincial boards, and war against Napoleon ensued with strong popular backing. On September 25, 1908, the provincial boards delegated their authority to a central board constituted in the palace of Aranjuez. In just six months, Aranjuez witnessed two crucial proofs of Spanish opposition to Napoleon, which preceded many other episodes that took place there during the convulsed nineteenth century in Spain.

On June 30, 1854, the so-called battle of Vicálvaro, near Madrid, ended in Aranjuez, where the cavalry of General O'Donell retreated after a brief exchange of fire with General Bláser's troops. This was more of a skirmish than a battle, one of the many that took place in the nineteenth century. Queen Isabel II is the central character of this period. Born in 1830, the daughter of Fernando VII, she lived in Aranjuez from 1843 to 1846, before her disastrous marriage to her cousin Francisco de Asís. There are fond recollections in her conversations and letters of her long strolls in the gardens of Aranjuez during her adolescent years. Later, as queen, she often went to the palace on the Tagus, and her quarters there, particularly the boudoir and the bedroom are faithfully maintained. In 1848 Isabel II inaugurated the Madrid-Aranjuez railway line, the third on Spanish soil (the first was in Havana and the second in Barcelona) and requested a station built in the trident so that she could go directly to the palace. On April 19, 1861, in Aranjuez, she signed the royal decree granting the petition by the independent Dominican Republic to return to Spanish sover-

eignty. The arrangement lasted only four years, but it was a very unusual one for a former colony.

On June 2, 1885, during the cholera epidemic that spread through most of Spain, King Alfonso XII (1857–1885), incognito and escorted by only one adjutant, took the train to Aranjuez, one of the areas where the disease was most virulent. The king visited every hospital and barracks filled with the sick and dying, and he met in the palace with the local and medical authorities. This gesture of sympathy to a suffering town was made by a king who was also ill. Alfonso XII died before the end of the year. This tragic event is offset by a comic episode. During a spring stay in Aranjuez in the 1890s, when Alfonso XIII was just a child, his mother the Queen Regent María Cristina punished his disobedience by locking him up in a room. The indignant and furious boy stuck his head out of a window and yelled, "Long live the Republic!"

Although Aranjuez was not far from the front lines during the Civil War, the palace was undamaged. Its temporary deterioration did not result from the war but from unplanned growth in the second half of the twentieth century. A large political and financial effort is underway to recover the qualities that made this place so attractive. In 1977 the palace was readied to receive foreign dignitaries while El Pardo was being renovated for this purpose over a five-year period. Many cultural and state functions continue to be held at Aranjuez, presided over by the king or the queen.

A distinguished biographer of Felipe II, Geoffrey Parker, relates that "when the royal family sailed down the Tagus, Felipe took a writing case with him on his launch and he continued to sign papers and resolve matters brought to him by his aide Ruiz de Velasco, while on the river banks the courtiers danced to the tune of a string orchestra." The king was probably not aware that for many centuries the essence of Aranjuez' magnetism was concentrated in that act: water, gardens, music, art, history, power, and royalty, the seven colors of the permanent spring of this royal site.

✠

The PALACE of
LA GRANJA de SAN ILDEFONSO

✠

The PALACE of
LA GRANJA de SAN ILDEFONSO

✠

A carefully selected site, a fidelity to certain traditional patterns, a prominently placed chapel, and an axial scheme are features of all Spanish palaces. La Granja de San Ildefonso has all of these, but with a particular history. Ortega y Gasset, the early twentieth-century Spanish thinker, said that "architecture is an enormous social gesture," and in this same vein the present author once wrote that El Escorial was an enormous gesture of Spanish architecture that reflects the power of Spain and Felipe II during the Counterreformation. One hundred sixty years later, something similar can be said about La Granja (The Farm) in the Province of Segovia, eighty kilometers north of Madrid, built by the first Spanish Bourbon king, Felipe V, from 1720 to 1740.

The Hapsburg king Carlos II died without issue in 1700, naming in his will a seventeen-year-old boy as heir to all the kingdoms and domains of the Spanish Crown. The boy was the Duke of Anjou, born at Versailles, a grandson of Louis XIV and grandnephew of King Felipe IV (father of the deceased King Carlos II). As king of Spain, Carlos II's heir is known as Felipe V de Borbón. His grandfather and supporter, Louis XIV, had uttered the startling proclamation that "there are no longer Pyrenees." England, the Low Countries, Portugal, Savoy, Prussia, and Austria found this Franco-Spanish alliance intolerable, and with the pretext of defending the rights of the pretender Archduke Karl of Austria—but actually to prevent such a fearsome tie—they launched a war that lasted thirteen years (1700–1713) in Spain itself as well as in Italy, the Rhine basin, and Flanders. The bloody war came to an end when Emperor Joseph I died and his brother Karl, the other pretender to the Spanish throne, inherited the Austrian empire. This created the poten-

tial of an alliance as frightful as the one the king's backers were trying to forestall.

Despite the fierce battles fought on Spanish soil during this war, some of them not far from the royal houses of the Austrian dynasty, Felipe V (1683–1746) and his family continued to live in these palaces. Although El Escorial was not much to the king's liking, he went there occasionally but lived mainly in the Alcázar of Madrid. At times he stayed at the Buen Retiro, where his first son was born on August 25, 1707. Because this is the feast day of Saint Louis King of France, the heir to the crown was named Luis. An adept hunter, the king also frequented the houses at El Pardo and Balsaín, accompanied by the Master of the Royal Horse and a large retinue.

The period from 1710 to 1715 was laden with decisive events in the king's political and family life. The War of Succession ended in 1713–1714 with the conclusion of the Treaty of Utrecht and several other accords, bringing a degree of calm to the political and military horizon of Felipe V. But these years were personally tragic for a man of his delicate temperament. In less than three years, he lost four members of his immediate family: in 1711 his father, the Grand Dauphin; in the following year his mother and his older brother Louis, another dauphin and Duke of Burgundy; and in 1713 his younger brother the Duke of Berry. The situation was critical because the crown of France had passed to the septuagenarian Louis XIV whose only heir was his nephew Louis, a sickly three-year-old child. Then, on Ash Wednesday, February 14, 1714, the Spanish queen, María Luisa Gabriela, died in El Pardo, leaving the king in a state of deep sorrow. Widowed at thirty-one, Felipe V could no longer be called The Spirited and came to earn the nickname of The Sad.

Louville said the king had "a strong but vaporous nature . . . nervous disturbances . . . clouds of sadness agitate him often, and thus, his intelligence seems engulfed and darkened."

Cardinal Acquaviva arranged a new marriage, this time to a princess from Parma, Isabella Farnese (in Spanish, Isabel de Farnesio). The marriage settlement was signed in Parma in August 1714, and the wedding Mass took place on Christmas Eve of the same year in the palace of the Duchy del Infantado in Guadalajara. The new queen, who deserved to have been called *the spirited*, soon launched her Italian objective: to expel the Austrians from Italy and to amend the stipulations of the Treaty of Utrecht. Felipe's mentor, Louis XIV, died at Versailles on September 1, 1715, ending a thorny chapter of family losses and political troubles in the king's life.

Professor Beatriz Blasco Esquivias, an expert on the evolution of La Granja palace, writes that although Felipe V showed strength and courage during the long War of Succession, the series of family losses concentrated in so few years drained his spirit forever: "These events accentuated the religious scruples of the monarch who, in his more neurasthenic periods, displayed psychotic behaviour . . . neglecting the affairs of State, soon to be taken over by his very new wife." The king's state moved him to an early abdication, and this is essential to an understanding of the creation of the palace of La Granja.

For several years Felipe V had counted on Teodoro Ardemans (1664–1726), head of royal building projects from 1702 and Architect of the King in 1703. Ardemans, a multitalented man—painter, sculptor, and above all an architect well versed in the late Madrilenian Baroque style—worked on the restoration and alterations of Madrid's Alcázar. In 1717 the king directed him to rebuild the Casa del Bosque in Balsaín, which had been abandoned since the 1682 fire and could be used for hunting parties.

The geography of this area is also important. The central Spanish tableland is divided in two by a mountain range that follows a southwest-northeast direction in the Segovian region. The Silla del Rey (King's Chair) is a wooded hill 1,609 meters high dominating a broad, long view of the northern Castilian tableland. The Balsaín palace is less than half a league away, in the foreground, and some three leagues beyond it are the spires and towers of the cathedral and

alcazar of Segovia. To the right, almost hidden by foliage and barely three kilometers away, a small farm could be seen. It stood on a gentle slope where the Balsaín and Cambrones streams flow and meet shortly below to form the Eresma River that runs at the foot of the city of Segovia. Inquiring about the farm, the king was told that it belonged to the Hieronymite friars of the Monastery of El Parral.

On the property there were also a small group of hunting houses and a shrine consecrated to San Ildefonso, built by the Trastámara king Enrique IV of Castilla (1425–1474). Legend has it that the saint saved the king from an attack by a wild animal while his party was hunting in the area. The Catholic sovereigns, Isabel and Fernando, donated the property to the monastery, and two centuries later the monastic order built a farm and a hostel on the older structures. Winter at that altitude is long and harsh but summer is very pleasant, and the monks used the hostel for short rest periods. This information changed the king's mind, and he ordered Ardemans to build a new house in this location, which put reconstruction of the Balsaín house aside. In March 1720 the king bought the land from the monks at El Parral and construction began in November, according to some authors, or the following spring according to others. Ardemans drew the plans for a modest building meant to be a vacation house rather than a palace, another Buen Retiro in the Segovian forest.

The new building was planned around the courtyard of the old hostel, with the same dimensions—16 by 16 meters—for the courtyard of the new house. The building was not going to be just a house, the gardens were and are integral to La Granja. Royal orders to fund the construction exist from 1721. Ardemans designed a rectangular house of approximately 63 by 58 meters, but the courtyard was not in the exact center. It was shifted toward the southwest, toward the main facade facing the gardens that French architect René Carlier (d. 1722) was designing at the same time.

The main facade could not face the south as Ardemans probably first intended because orienting the building to the four cardinal points on that smooth slope would have involved enormous and very costly regrading. Therefore the southwest-northeast axis of the building paralleled the mountains crests and the southeast-northwest axis followed the direction of the slope. Since La Granja's site was approached from

Balsaín along the Balsaín River, it was natural to place the main facade and entrance gate on the southwest, while the northeast side was given over to service yards, including parking for carriages. This space is still called the Patio de Carruajes (Carriage Courtyard). The main rooms were placed in the southeast wing to take advantage of the sunshine and the magnificent vistas of the gardens.

Inevitably, the northwest facade, which looked down the slope toward Segovia, was the location for the dominant element in all Spanish palaces, the chapel. Centering the chapel on the northwest facade, with a large volume marking the layout, was not only an Ardemans decision. The king knew that the chapel of his new house could not have a lateral, relatively secondary position as did the chapel at Versailles. The chapel had to stand out, filling one of the axes of the layout as it did at El Escorial and as Felipe V later situated the chapel in the Royal Palace of Madrid. If he did not do this at El Pardo, it was because the building was already there and placing the chapel in the center would have involved prohibitively complex architectural surgery.

With these premises, Ardemans erected the palace in little more than three years. Not only was he the king's architect but also the municipal architect of his birthplace, Madrid. In this capacity, he was well acquainted with the architectural language of the second half of the seventeenth century. The style of this period, or rather the substyle, is sometimes known as Madrilenian Baroque. This language derives from the Alcázar: granite plinths, window frames, and other trim; brick walls in reddish or purple-brown tones; stone cornices; and towers with pyramidal slate spires. The Palace of La Granja had this look about 1724, and it still can be seen in the northwest facade, which is the least altered side of the building. Ardemans, whose talent for arranging spaces was well proven, was a distant disciple of Gómez de Mora and Carbonell. Thus some of their work in Madrid churches, the court jail and the Alcázar can be felt through Ardemans in La Granja.

The basic plan of La Granja was that of the traditional castle, or rather of the Spanish alcazar, but with some novelties wisely incorporated by Ardemans. La Granja had four towers, 9 by 9 meters each, with slate spires that were not precisely in the corners. They were set back on diagonals, forming a faceted elevation and a strange arrangement of roof slopes and hips. A clear precedent was the Torre de la Parada in El Pardo forest, but here with a wider ground floor. José Luis Sancho wittily calls this shape a "hoop skirt," a design that Ardemans used for the four La Granja towers. With the entrance to the palace on the southwest, shifting the courtyard toward that facade allowed carriages to go directly to the northeast yard, bypassing the fountain in the center of the main courtyard. This Fountain Courtyard had five open arches and pilasters on each side of the ground floor and balconies on the first story.

Was such simplicity forced by the unadorned nature of the monks' farm? This seems too easy an explanation. Rather, the design of the pilasters, brackets, and lintels of the upper floor probably shows that the architect dominated the clean idiom of his native Madrid Baroque. Others try to explain the location of the church as a reminiscence of the castle keep, but this too seems an exaggeration. More likely the architect inserted the church, with its full importance, at a prominent place in the masterfully laid out arrangement. This church is similar in plan and proportions to the Alpajés church, in the western part of the town of Aranjuez, created by Ardemans at almost the same time. Needless to say, the dominant feature of the palace was not the four towers but the octagonal dome over the church transept. Looking at the building from any angle, the dome always commanded the view of the whole.

Doubt remains as to whether the northeast stairway was originally placed there by Ardemans or was added later. From a functional standpoint, Ardemans may have planned a stairway there but of a different design than the present one. What is unlikely, considering the harsh winters of La Granja, is that there were any rooms in the stairway area. This supports the opinions of Beatriz Blasco Esquivias and Yves Bottineau, who claim that the entrance to the palace was on the Balsaín side, the natural access to La Granja. Some unique features in this part of the building, such as the elliptical two-story hall centered on the entrance, may even have been part of Ardemans's design to enhance such an essential element of the palace as its entrance.

The king and queen moved to La Granja in the autumn of 1723. The designer René Carlier had died the year before, but the gardens were in the good hands of Etienne Boutelou and Etienne Marchand. All was going according to schedule, when the king's sudden decision surprised everyone, although he had been considering it for some time. After Cardinal Borja consecrated the palace church on Christmas 1723, the court was expected to return to Madrid. But Felipe V lingered for some days at La Granja to announce to his closest advisers that he planned to abdicate the Spanish Crown. At only forty-one, he left the throne to his son Luis, prince of Asturias, who reigned as Luis I de Borbón. The ex-king retired to La Granja to rest after ruling Spain for almost a quarter century.

Felipe V's second wife, Isabel, did not feel exactly as he did: the crown of Spain had gone to her stepson Luis, but her husband maintained full rights to the French Crown; if his sickly nephew Louis XV should die, Felipe would be proclaimed king and she could then be queen of France. But history had it another way. Louis XV survived Felipe V by twenty-eight years and his niece Isabel by eight, and Luis I de Borbón died seven months after ascending the throne. Felipe V had to take back the crown with all its consequences. He immediately proclaimed his second son heir to the throne, and although this son was only eleven years old, a wife had to be found for him to assure his succession.

But while the state machinery worked to secure the continuity of the monarchy, another smaller and more personal machine was active in other endeavors. Felipe V was not ready to give up La Granja de San Ildefonso, where he had placed so many hopes and spent so much money. It was absolutely necessary to reconvert the vacation retreat into a royal palace by enlarging and enriching it. A total change of image was inevitably underway.

Felipe V's urgent petition to Rome resulted in the papal bull *Deum Infatigabilem*, issued by the recently elected Orsini Pope, Benedict XIII, granting the chapel of La Granja the status of Collegiate Church. The most brilliant aspect of the new La Granja was to be the main facade, the one facing the gardens. Ardemans died early in 1726 and another architect had to be summoned. He was the Italian Andrea Procaccini (1671–1734), the second great architect of La Granja. (Filippo Juvarra did not intervene until 1735.) Born in Rome, Procaccini came to Spain in 1720 as a painter to Felipe V. In

1723 he was at work on the Marble Sitting Room in the front wing of La Granja and thus was well acquainted with the building he had to enlarge. The design for this expansion was well known, and Francesco Sabbatini used it a century later in Aranjuez and Madrid. It consisted of attaching two wings to the towered corners of the original rectangle. The corners could not be those facing the gardens or those on the northwest. This would have engulfed the church and altered its lateral accesses. The slope was sharper there, too, which prevented the desired continuity of the additions. The logical choice was to expand horizontally, and Procaccini designed two parallel wings emerging from the Balsaín facade and two more in the northeast direction. The wings were 45 meters long and a little over 10 meters wide, increasing the main facade facing the gardens from 63 meters to approximately 153. La Granja was expanded from a royal country house to a great European palace.

But Procaccini's additions were not identical. Rather similar in their geometry, they had very distinct faces. The first wings built were those extending to the northeast. The one looking into the gardens was double in height to accommodate the Hall of the Ambassadors, and it was to house the sculpture collection brought from the heirs of Queen Christina of Sweden. When the parallel back wing was erected, a U-shaped yard was formed. This was the Carriage Yard for parking carriages that entered from the northwest, either from Balsaín or Segovia, so that travelers could descend inside the new courtyard just in front of the main stairway. These alterations were carried out from the end of 1724 to the beginning of 1727. The two wings that grew to the southwest were constructed next, forming another U-shaped courtyard but with a curved facade at the bottom of the U. It was soon called Patio de la Herradura (Horseshoe Courtyard).

During the construction, the royal family carried on their normal life in the palace. Infanta María Teresa, who was to marry the French dauphin, was born there in 1726 as was the Infante Luis Antonio in 1727.

Procaccini was assisted by Sempronio Subisati (c. 1690–1758), who was placed in charge of the Horseshoe Courtyard construction. This area connected with the original southwest corner to a new Casa de Oficios through a three-arch passageway (named the Infante's, or

San José's, or Franco's) that had already been built at the west of the main building to replace the older one that was no longer adequate. But aside from enlarging the palace these additions by Procaccini and Subisati were intended to somehow mask Ardemans's Collegiate Church. This chapel was judged too bare, too orthogonal and alcazar-like, too much like Felipe IV of Austria in relation to the Italianate idiom of the Horseshoe Courtyard. Thus the Italians, Procaccini and Subisati, set out to Italianize the church exterior in 1727.

It was not easy, but Procaccini, who had apprenticed in Rome to the painter Carlo Maratta, had the experience and ability to meet the challenge. The aesthetic ideas of Annibale Carracci reached La Granja through Procaccini and his Roman master. In front of the church wall Procaccini added a floor with towers at both ends, towers with belfry lanterns, pediments, and octagonal domes ending in thin needles. The curving center wall was very much in keeping with seventeenth-century Roman churches, and together with the large transept dome, achieved an attractive perspective. Procaccini's talent converted the stern protruding wall of the church into a sumptuous motif, on which the architect José Díaz Gamones based subsequent works. This was the background for what has been known for two centuries as the Plaza del Palacio (Palace Plaza).

Procaccini died in 1734, the year of the fire in the Alcázar of Madrid. This fire led to the arrival of Filippo Juvarra (1678–1736) to design a new royal palace in Madrid. Juvarra's prestige was so great that while his major task was the new palace the king suggested that he also look after the completion of La Granja. Subisati had been put in charge of La Granja, but he did not remain for very long. Subisati had been working with Procaccini for some months on the alteration and embellishment of the garden facade that was now over 150 meters long. Since the Ardemans-designed center section was set back relative to the recently added side wings, an arcade supporting a long balcony and the original cornices was justified. The king put the solution to this disunity between the center building and the two wings in Juvarra's hands. Juvarra's design yielded a pictorial and coloristic effect far superior to anything Procaccini could have produced. The order and rhythm of the facade, combining white marble with pink Sepúlveda limestone, make this one of the best eighteenth-century

facades in Spain—indeed in Europe. The rectangular attic, with three panels and a balustrade, in the opinion of many authors, bests the New Palace of Madrid, and of course, other palaces, such as the Liria, which is very much in the manner of Juvarra, designed by Ventura Rodríguez. But, as Professor Ortega and scholar José Luis Sancho have recently shown, what we see now is an alteration, and an improvement, made by Juvarra's pupil Sacchetti, who once again was able to transfer his teacher's concepts from paper to stone.

If Juvarra had kept the original Ardemans alignment that front would have been set back, but the able hand of his successor Gianbattista Sacchetti (1697–1784) made it flush with the side wings with no loss of beauty or strength. This was the only way to save the three halls in that central section, precisely where the throne room was to be placed and in later alterations the king and queen's antechambers and bedrooms. Ardemans's facade no longer exists, and it is not known whether Sacchetti's foundations removed its underpinning or whether it was intentionally demolished. The fact is that the garden front is now uniform and beautiful, thanks to Sacchetti who improved the work of Ardemans and Procaccini through the distant and genial hand of Juvarra. The gallery in the wing between the garden and the carriage yard is also Sacchetti's. This was spoiled in the nineteenth century by an intermediate floor added to build the quarters for the queen's consort Don Francisco de Asís far away from the queen's apartment.

Filippo Juvarra must be thanked for bringing his friend the painter Giovanni Paolo Panini (1691/92–1765) to Spain. Panini was commissioned to paint four panels for the rooms in the southernmost rooms looking to the gardens, where the Mirror Room for Isabel de Farnesio was situated (now the Music Room). He also painted four panels for the royal bedroom designed by Juvarra, with orientalized pilasters and lacquered carvings. The subject of Panini's panels was the public life of Jesus, and the artist showed himself to be the best composer of architectural backgrounds of the eighteenth century, even exceeding Rubens in this ability some experts believe.

By about 1740 the palace had been admirably converted into the seat of the court. It was growing toward Segovia with buildings that shaped the symmetrical Palace Plaza, such as the Casa de Oficios de Canónigos (Canons), the stables, and the barracks. This urban fabric was completed by Carlos III, who also originated the royal site as we know it today. The Palace Plaza was landscaped under Isabel II, and the huge sequoias were planted during the regency of Queen María Cristina.

The gardens, like the palace, were not all made at one time. The central area, the New Cascade in front of the palace, is a *jardin de propieté* inspired by the gardens at Marly. The landscape designer Carlier placed the Queen's Pavilion, or sewing room, at the end of the perspective, flanking the axes with fountains, statues, and flower beds. The area to the right called the "park," is more rustic, organized on two strong diagonals stemming from the plaza of the Eight Streets. The axis toward Balsaín is adorned with a flower bed and a fountain, both named La Fama (Fame). The fountain sends a powerful jet of water into the air, since it is much lower than the ponds that feed it. And then there are the other fountains: the Labyrinth, La Selva (The Forest), and the outstanding powerful architecture of the fountain called Diana's Bath. Hubert Dumandré, Pierre Pitué, and Jean Thierry worked on the garden statuary, but René Frémin (1672–1744) deserves special mention for his exceptional busts of Felipe, Isabel, and Luis. This dynamic garden became the most beautiful display imaginable in the eighteenth century.

King Felipe V died in 1746 in Madrid at the age of sixty-three, and Isabel, the ambitious, energetic queen, at Aranjuez in 1766. Both rest in the sacristy of the Collegiate Church they built. The sepulcher was probably designed by Ferdinando Fuga (1699–1784). They were interred in their beloved home, the modest retreat they had made into a grand palace surrounded by the most splendid fountains and magnificent gardens in Europe. La Granja became a center of power and a repository of history for subsequent centuries.

In September 1765 La Granja was the stage for the wedding of Prince Carlos, later King Carlos IV, and María Luisa de Parma, a marriage that the historian Marquis de Lozoya (1893–1978) characterized as ill-starred, because the naiveté of Carlos and the indiscretions of María Luisa threw the Spanish crown into precipitous decline. Both the king and the queen died in exile in Rome within a few weeks of each other. Also at La Granja, the Treaty of San Ildefonso between Spain and France was signed, a treaty filled with misfortune for Spain. The defeats of San Vicente and Trafalgar and the absurd Orange War with Portugal were but a foretaste of the Peninsular War of 1808 engendered by this treaty.

The so-called episodes of La Granja were not happier. In 1832, when Fernando VII was very ill, the Royal Minister Tadeo Calomarde, using all sorts of schemes and half truths, managed to persuade the king to sign a decree voiding the Pragmatic Sanction, a document the king had signed two years earlier making a 1789 decision of Parliament fully valid. That decision entitled women to ascend the Spanish throne. Calomarde's intent was to prevent either the older daughter of the king, Isabel, then two years old, or the younger, Luisa Fernanda, eight months old, from becoming queen. This would ensure that the crown would pass to the king's brother Carlos, who headed a movement called Carlism. Fernando VII recovered just as his brother Francisco de Paula rushed into the palace with his Neapolitan wife, Luisa Carlota, who before witnesses tore up the document signed by the misled king, and, reproving Calomarde for his evil act, slapped him. Calomarde, downcast, replied, "White hands do not offend," a response that has entered history. This episode, nonetheless, did not change the fact that clearing Isabel's path to the throne made the Carlist Wars inevitable. Four years later, the sergeants of La Granja garrison mutinied to force the Queen Regent María Christina to reenact the 1812 Constitution.

During the reigns of Isabel II, Alfonso XII, and María Christina of Hapsburg, La Granja continued to be the royal summer residence, because its climate 1,200 meters above sea level is cooler than the warm Castilian plains. In the early twentieth century Alfonso XIII and Victoria Eugenia (Ena) of Battenberg honeymooned at La Granja and three of their children were born there, each in June, during the royal family summer season: Don Jaime (1908), Doña Beatriz (1909), and Don Juan (1913), the father of King Juan Carlos I. Don Juan celebrated his seventy-fifth birthday in the central hall of La Granja, which carries his name and is presided over by his bust.

On January 2, 1918, fire destroyed a large part of La Granja's roofs, including the church and other buildings, such as the Casa de Damas. Fire-fighting operations took eight days, because of frozen water pipes and a fierce blizzard. The repair work, under architect Juan Moya, lasted more than nine years. The old architectural forms were faithfully reproduced, but steel members were substituted for wood. Unfortunately, there were insufficient funds to rebuild the Pharmacy House, with its Botica, La Parra, and Chico courtyards. It was replaced by a simpler building with the same front to the plaza as the building the fire had destroyed. The tapestry collection is now shown here.

La Granja's star declined after the fire and the lengthy reconstruction. With the proclamation of the Republic in 1931, the royal family went into exile. President Alcalá Zamora was against building a new presidential palace or purchasing any of the palaces offered by the aristocracy. He established his official office in the Royal Palace of Madrid, which was then renamed the National Palace. After a rapid, superficial repair, the president spent the summer of 1932 at La Granja. This is the impression he reflected with sadness in his *Memoirs:* "It was decided that La Granja will be the president's summer residence . . . because of its proximity to Madrid. . . . When the summer of 1932 came and I went there to install myself, I was astonished to find the palace dismantled." Indeed, the rich furniture that Alcalá knew well (he was a crown minister twice) and miraculously saved from the fire, could not be saved from the Minister of Defense Azaña, who ordered it secretly moved to the official residences of the prime minister and his own.

Some years later, during the Civil War, La Granja was the scene of a brief but dangerous battle. In May 1937, the new Republican cabinet, presided over by Juan Negrín with Indalecio Prieto at the Ministry of War, decided to launch an offensive to relieve the pressure applied by the Rebels against Bilbao in the north. The attack began on May 30, when the 31st Brigade descended from high ground toward the gardens of La Granja. Two battalions charged against the main facade, defended by an improvised company of civilian volunteers behind sand bags placed in the windows and balconies. A sally by the defenders secured the Queen's Arbor. One battalion of the 31st Brigade enveloped the palace from the north to avoid a frontal clash. Luckily, the artillery shelling and air bombing missed the palace, which was only hit by light-weapons fire. The vanguard battalion of

the 31st Brigade cut the Torrecaballeros road. This broke the Francoist front between the Atalaya hill and the Glass Factory, a building designed by Villanueva in the eighteenth century. Another battalion stormed the palace gardens and was repulsed by a line from the Andrómeda and Canastillo (Little Basket) fountains. The next day the 14th Brigade replaced the 31st and the center of the attack shifted to the southwest relieving the pressure on the palace. The 31st insisted on enveloping the palace on the north, but they were stopped by an artillery battery on Matabueyes hill. Two days later the Republicans withdrew and their propaganda described the operation as a successful local attack. Propaganda aside, the palace and gardens suffered little damage. The marble and pink stone facade and the fenestration and glass panes were repaired in the 1940s. Only some marks of rifle shots and shrapnel in the ironwork remind us of that happily forgotten battle.

The Palace of La Granja, after being the scene of monarchical and Republican events, was also the place where General Franco celebrated the anniversaries of the start of the Civil War every July 18. He also used to fish in the nearby streams and stayed for some days in the rooms over the San José Arch (also called Franco's Arch), rehabilitated in the 1940s by his architect Diego Méndez.

Today the Palace of La Granja contains within its stylistically varied facades a museum showing a notable sample of paintings and sculpture, aside from the garden sculpture. If the sculptures bought from the heirs of the Swedish Crown had remained in La Granja, the Juvarra gallery facing the garden would house the best sculpture collection in Spain. But these royal collections have enriched others at their own expense. El Prado Museum, for instance, is indebted to La Granja for its sculpture collection.

The paintings now exhibited at La Granja are superb, even though some of the best ones were moved to the Prado Museum and to other royal palaces. The four Paninis have already been mentioned, but the works of Louis-Michel van Loo (1707–1771) are equally excellent. Van Loo, together with Michel-Ange Houasse (1680–1730) and Jean Ranc (1674–1735), are the French painters that came to Spain at the time of Felipe V. Van Loo was trained in Paris, Turin, and Rome, and he arrived in Spain in 1737, worked for Felipe V and his son Fernando VI and was the teacher of the well-known still-life painter Luis Meléndez (1716–1780). Van Loo idealized Felipe V and Isabel in separate portraits, but his dramatic, luxurious portrait of the royal family is probably the second best of that genre in the Spanish eighteenth century—only after Goya's *Family of Carlos IV.*

What truly deserves a trip to La Granja is the tapestry collection, shown in the building created by Moya and Durán after the 1918 fire. It is difficult to describe the enormous pleasure a sensitive viewer feels in front of the best tapestries in the world. The Van Aelst series *The Honours,* *The Apocalypse,* and *The Triumphs of Petrarch* make La Granja an altar to the cult of this art. The well-known Hispanist Jonathan Brown commented one day without taking his eyes from *Divine Wisdom,* one of The Honours series: "To own a tapestry in the sixteenth century was like owning a Rolls-Royce in the twentieth century, a luxury, a richness within reach of very few. Collections such as these could only be possessed by the most powerful monarchs of Europe."

✛

The PALACE of RIOFRÍO

✛

The PALACE of RIOFRÍO

✠

Tradition attributes the origin of the Palace of Riofrío to the spite of a stepmother, Isabel de Farnesio, Queen of Spain. Isabel saw the doors of the Spanish court close to her and her children on the death of her husband, Felipe V, in 1746. Luis, the king's son by his first wife, María Luisa Gabriela of Savoy, succeeded his father. As a consequence, Isabel ordered a new palace built in Riofrío for herself, to avoid encumbering another stepson at the court, Fernando VI, and his wife, Bárbara de Braganza. Her move would avoid the discomforts arising from matters of protocol and precedence. This spite of a stepmother—or better characterized, her flight to avoid feeling uneasy or rejected—is quite credible. More recent studies on the origin of Riofrío add another reason, as reasonable as it is simple. By building the Palace of Riofrío, Isabel de Farnesio was creating a suitable residence for one of her children, the only child who was left relatively "displaced." The palace was for her and her beloved son Luis Antonio Jaime. To analyze this case of motherly love requires a brief acquaintance with the children of Isabel and Felipe V and their royal destiny in eighteenth-century Europe.

In 1714 Isabella Farnese Neuberg-Bayern, then twenty-two years old, was married to King Felipe V of Spain. The fate of their issue is impressive. Isabel managed to place Carlos, born in 1716, in the kingdom of Naples as Carlos VII. Years later, on the death of his stepbrother Fernando VI in 1759, he took over the throne of Spain as Carlos III. His return to the court of Madrid strengthened Isabel's position as Queen Mother and led to the total abandonment of the unfinished palace at Riofrío.

In 1717 Isabel gave birth to another child, Francisco, who lived only five weeks. A year later the Infanta María Ana Victoria was born.

Affectionately nicknamed *la Marianina*, she became queen of Portugal through her marriage to José I of Bragança, first son of the famous Joao V the Magnanimous. The fourth child of the royal couple, Felipe, born in 1720, was made Duke of Parma and Piacenza. He married the firstborn child of Louis XV of France, Louise, a marriage that began the Italian dynasty of Bourbon-Parma. In 1726 Isabel gave birth to another child, the Infanta María Teresa Antonia, who married the dauphin, son of Louis XV in 1745.

The sixth child of Felipe V and Isabel was born in 1727 and named Luis Antonio Jaime. This infante becomes the key figure in the origin of the Palace of Riofrío. The last child of the royal couple was born November 17, 1729. Christened María Antonia Fernanda, she married Vittorio Amedeo III of Savoy, king of Sardinia, in 1749.

This was the extraordinarily able marriage policy Isabel de Farnesio pursued for their children. In principle, all were called to be second-line infantes in a difficult search for accommodation in European courts as stepbrothers and sisters of Fernando VI.

Was the Infante Luis Antonio left "unemployed"? Not at all, his mother also made sure that Don Luis Antonio Jaime de Borbón y Farnesio had an enviable position. Through the minister José Patiño, Isabel obtained the office of administrator of the temporal wealth of the archdiocese of Toledo for Luis Antonio when he was only eight years old; and when he was fourteen he was given the same office in Sevilla. In the 1730s he was made a cardinal by Pope Clement XII with the title of Santa María della Scala.

Luis Antonio was not the first cardinal in the Spanish court. A century earlier, Pope Paul V Borghese had made Felipe IV's brother Fernando a cardinal. Fernando had discharged this church position with dignity, and in addition he became an excellent soldier. But Luis Antonio did not feel the slightest ecclesiastic, political, or military vocation. All of this had been arranged by the powerful Isabel and facilitated by Patiño and by the inevitable Annibale de Scotti, who administered the opulent income of the Toledan cardinalate. Scotti himself even managed to participate in the spiritual rule of the archdiocese through a government board he controlled at will.

Luis Antonio retained the rank of cardinal for almost nineteen years, but he remained at the court throughout his adolescence and young manhood. There is no evidence that he ever visited Toledo. In December 1754, when the infante was twenty-seven years old, he resigned the offices at Toledo and Sevilla as well as that of cardinal. These resignations took place exactly two years after the building of the palace at Riofrío began. This reinforces the idea that Riofrío was intended for Luis Antonio more than for Isabel. But the death of his stepbrother Fernando VI in 1759 and the return of his brother to become Carlos III precipitated events. It strengthened the position of Isabel and Luis Antonio at the court of Madrid, which led to the gradual decline of the building project at Riofrío.

In 1775 Luis Antonio requested permission from his brother King Carlos III to marry, in order to "guarantee his eternal salvation." The permission granted, he took as his wife, in a morganatic marriage, a young Saragossan aristocrat, María Teresa Villabriga y Rozas. This put an end to the infante's love affairs and courtly adventures. The couple led a peaceful life in Velada, then in Cadalso, and finally in Arenas de San Pedro, where Luis Antonio built a palace based on plans by Ventura Rodríguez. Rodríguez was then enjoying great professional success, with commissions from the Council of Castilla, the Church, and the nobility. At Arenas de San Pedro, Goya painted at least two portraits of Luis Antonio with his wife and children.

Construction at Riofrío began in 1752. The palace was designed by a fine Italian architect, Virgilio Rabaglio (1711–1811), born in Gandria, who came to Spain as Gianbattista Sacchetti's assistant for the construction of the Royal Palace in Madrid and then received other court-related commissions. Rabaglio was a competent, experienced designer and builder, considering not only his brief early practice in Italy but also the fifteen years he worked in Spain before being entrusted with Riofrío. For this job he had both a great advantage and what later proved to be a great disadvantage. The advantage was his well-proven capacity as an architect and his long experience in building, acquired with the large job in Madrid, the one at Aranjuez, the new Caños del Peral Theater near Madrid's New Palace, and with various engineering projects.

But Rabaglio's fine talent was shadowed by a negative trait. He was what today is called an obedient architect. Rabaglio obeyed Scotti, the man who enjoyed Isabel's full confidence; and the powerful marquis did not hesitate to choose Rabaglio to design Riofrío. This allowed Scotti to do there what he could not do in Madrid, where the architect Sacchetti adamantly resisted the dictates of the marquis. In Riofrío the situation was quite different, since with Rabaglio's compliance, both the architecture and its decoration would emerge to Scotti's taste. And this is what happened. The new palace was built to the image and likeness of the Madrilenian model, but it was smaller and less adorned, although with fine, elegant lines.

The cornerstone of the north facade, near the chapel, was laid in October 1752, in the presence of the Cardinal Infante Luis Antonio. But Scotti had died in February of that year and Rabaglio lost his protector. His fall was only a matter of time, the time his followers needed to gather all the technical documents and drawings in order to work without him. A team of ex-collaborators headed by Carlo Fraschina (d. 1754), who was paid a lower fee than Rabaglio and was quite inferior to him in talent and expertise, took over the project with limited authority to design and control a job of this size. Fortunately, Fraschina did not alter Rabaglio's plans, probably because he lacked the talent or ability to do so. No doubt he also wanted to avoid any future disagreements with Queen Isabel, who was pleased with the original design her faithful Scotti had approved.

The petty political maneuver that expelled Rabaglio from Riofrío is unfortunate. While he was not a genius, he had solid training in architecture, engineering, and construction, which would have made him equally inventive in enriching and improving his original drawings as the project developed. In the second four-year construction stage, from 1753 to 1757 under Fraschina and his team, the building was raised 15 meters and the vaults of the main level were closed.

The event that brought quality to Riofrío at this stage was the arrival of French architect Jaime Marquet (c. 1710—1782) to the site. He was an experienced designer who worked in the royal houses, particularly at Aranjuez. The imprint he left in Riofrío can be seen in the elegant curved panels of the doors, in the woodwork, and the well-conceived balustrades of the stairways.

The last stage under José Díaz Gamones runs from 1757 to 1766. Díaz was a master able to pull together the palace entrance axis from a city planning point of view. In the middle of this nine-year period, Isabel de Farnesio's stepson King Fernando VI died, a widower without children, and the return of her son Carlo VII of Naples as Carlos III reopened the doors of the court. Thus Riofrío no longer deserved the Queen Mother's attention. Although palace construction stretched out until 1766, it was not trouble-free during the erection of the east wing and the future parade ground.

On July 11, 1766, Isabel de Farnesio died in Aranjuez at the age of seventy-three, sickly, in pain, and almost blind. The Riofrío palace was completed with part of her inheritance. The west wing required a formidable stone foundation to overcome the sharp gradient of the terrain. Amazingly, this was built but the wing was not. This construction today is called *las murallas* (the ramparts) or *los murallones* (the great ramparts).

No stonework exists in the entire province of Segovia (except for the aqueduct) that is so impressive in its magnitude and the amount of labor involved. *Los murallones* is a true monument to an unfinished project, to foundations with nothing built on them, planned just to compensate for a few meters of difference in level.

Perhaps it is better this way. If the plaza at the south of the palace had been built, we would never be able to appreciate the true value of this colossal rampart. There is still another unfinished monument, built to connect the west facade and the new wing that was to form the plaza. It remains isolated now, just a stump housing a helicoid stairway. By its very nature—an incomplete, unsupported construction—it is a lesson on work well done and an evocation of an elegant, romantic ruin of what could have been.

About 1770 the Palace of Riofrío must have looked very much like it does today: a great palace in the Italian style, a perfect square,

84 by 84 meters, erected on a low flat hill at the south end of the Riofrío forest. Arriving at the site from the northeast, the road winds as it climbs and Riofrío is seen as a full-scale model, cold, elegant, and bare. Arriving from the south and entering through the Madrid gate, the plaza looks strangely open, missing the west wing that was never built.

At an altitude of 1,054 meters above sea level, Riofrío fits its name. The hard and long winter tints the sky gray during those months to become azure in spring, providing the best backdrop to the fine, rosy stuccoed facade with fenestration of a "faded apple green," according to Don Juan López de Contreras, Marquis of Lozoya, the Segovian aristocrat and scholar. The marquis is one of the men who knew Riofrío best and did the most to preserve it in recent decades.

Many say the history of Riofrío is short and sad, and for some even nonexistent, but this is not true. It is one of the Spanish palaces most closely identified with its singular fate. If Riofrío during the eighteenth century was above all an illusion suddenly overshadowed by greater causes, in the nineteenth it was the venue of royal solitude, of two misunderstandings and two sentimental tragedies, a falling out of love and a widowhood. This requires an explanation in terms of the architecture of the palace.

The square plan of Riofrío has a square inner courtyard as well, 30.7 meters on each side. The basic scheme of the building derives directly from the Royal Palace in Madrid, but with the changes Scotti wanted to incorporate there and Sacchetti's obstinacy prevented. These changes were finally included at Riofrío thanks to the malleable, obedient Rabaglio.

The facades are oriented to the four cardinal points. The main front with the royal entrance faces south. This entry follows the superb scheme the Royal Palace of Madrid could have had: a great vestibule that allowed carriages to stop at the foot of a double imperial stairway ascending to the stately main floor. More modest but nonetheless elegant are the secondary entrances at the east and west facades, which also give access to the central courtyard. The royal chapel is elliptical in shape and situated on the north side, as in Madrid, but it is cramped because of the squeezed-in size limitations of the bay.

If the Riofrío scheme follows Sacchetti's design for Madrid, it is executed in a contained, restrained manner, in a minor key. The square plan presents setoffs in the corners, somewhat reminiscent of the turreted alcazar, as an elegant geometric abstraction. This may be one of the key ideas of this palace: its geometry and the graphic rationalism that is involved in such geometry. While its basic layout may be the same as that of the Madrid palace, Riofrío has a strict, flat geometry, both in plan an elevation, softened only by very light Italianate touches.

The arrangement of the main, secondary, and even tertiary stairways reveals an extraordinary geometric discipline. The secondary stairways are of a rational order that deserves mention: there is one landing every five steps, and twenty steps make a full turn. Fifty risers, or two-and-a-half turns, give access to the first story, with a total height of 7.34 meters. Next, with the same plan of ten five-step stretches the stair climbs another 7.34 meters and leads to the second story, 14.68 meters above ground. In sum, one hundred steps to climb to that height, which means a very comfortable riser of 14.68 centimeters.

The elevations show the same geometrical rigor. A powerful three-course granite lower level. A ground floor finished in rose stucco, with very classical vertical openings, varied and bordered with stone, ending in a shallow cornice. The first floor openings are somewhat more ornamented, with alternating triangular and arched pediments. The building resembles a seventeenth-century Roman palace with its main story topped with another shallow horizontal adornment to link it with the upper story. The upper level contains the service quarters and the openings are simpler but within the same strict order.

Crowning it all is the parapet with alternate closed and baluster sections, following the rhythm imposed by the facade. And finally the ornaments, flowered vases of Sepúlveda limestone in a rose tone finish off the vertical axes.

Riofrío is more than a simplified version of the Royal Palace in Madrid. It has its own personality and charm. The simple decorative motifs are very much its own. Within this relative bareness, there are very fine details, such as the pilasters of the inner courtyard and the high lyre-shaped openings of the half-round arches on the main floor. The palace is order and harmony in a discrete tone, and its exceptional location, doubtlessly chosen by Rabaglio, may make the building a foreign element in the middle of a forest of holm oaks and cedars. In its two centuries of life, however, it seems to have blended with the landscape and become an integral part of the scenery.

The singularity of its architecture, its remoteness from urban centers, the hospitable feeling created by its well-proportioned vaults, is perhaps what made Riofrío an ideal retirement place for two kings of Spain.

In the mid-nineteenth century Queen Isabel II's consort, King Francisco de Asís de Borbón (1822–1902), often retreated to his private apartment in the Palace of Riofrío because of their chronic disagreements. Don Francisco must have been a man highly sensitive to the arts and music, an intelligent and cultivated prince, qualities found infrequently among the nineteenth-century royalty. His daughter, the Infanta Eulalia de Borbón, used to say that he had an uncommon natural goodness and finesse, and that his delicate, expressive hands were the clearest sign of his great sensitivity.

A visitor to Riofrío should walk through the main floor of the palace to evoke the unhappy figure of King Francisco, whose spirit seems to wander through his rooms in the west wing. In the one named Cámara de Don Francisco (Don Francisco's Chamber) there are two excellent bronze busts on a pair of Parisian chests of drawers, one of Isabel II, depicted with the extraordinarily expressive force of her vigorous face and the other of her husband, King Francisco, very handsome in his uniform, with the Golden Fleece around his neck. Looking at the bronze eyes of this bust one gets a glimpse of the prolonged tragedy of this man who cured his forsakenness in the Palace of Riofrío.

The other figure at Riofrío in the second half of the nineteenth century is Don Francisco's heir, King Alfonso XII (1857–1885). Alfonso's stays at Riofrío to rest and hunt were frequent. He spent his most tragic days there in July 1878, just a few weeks after he lost his first wife and blood cousin, María de las Mercedes. The couple had had an extraordinary royal marriage of only five months, strengthened by the sincere love they felt for each other. The queen's death and the king's loss were mourned by the people, and soon the event became folk legend in verses and songs.

Very shortly before 1878, however, Riofrío must have been the scene of Alfonso XII's love affair with one of his most faithful lovers, Elena Sanz, whom he knew from the time of his stay in Vienna. The echoes of Riofrío's short history died with Alfonso's death in November 1885. His steward, Ceferino Rodríguez, who accompanied him closely during all of his stays at the Segovian palace, honored the fidelity required by his position, and there is almost no further documentation of Alfonso's period at Riofrío. When the palace reopened as a museum in June 1965, by initiative of the Marquis of Lozoya, the restored and refurnished rooms were fittingly named Museo Alfonsino in memory of that Spanish monarch whose reign was brief but significant and who confessed to being both Catholic and liberal.

In the early decades of the twentieth century, Riofrío recovered a certain historical rhythm when another Alfonso, the young Prince of Asturias, whose life was also tragic, resided at times in the palace to pursue his interests in livestock breeding and agriculture. Another visitor of royal standing was Don Juan, the count of Barcelona and father of the present King Don Juan Carlos. The count went to Riofrío especially to inspect the installation of the royal family's hunting trophies. Since July 1970 the north and west wings on the first floor of the palace have been given over to the Museum of the Hunt. Hunting is an activity dear to many Spanish royal houses. This museum alone, with its display of historic hunting memorabilia, justifies a visit to the Segovian palace. Several halls on the ground floor contain excellent hunting trophies of the royal family, and the collection continues to grow with objects brought back just yesterday, as it were.

In one of these halls there is an excellent equestrian portrait of young Alfonso XIII painted by Ramón Casas. It is among the best works of twentieth-century art in the royal painting collection.

Although Riofrío's history is colored by nostalgia and evocation, the royal collections contain excellent objects. Among these are some remarkable and valuable etchings, and the most outstanding pictures are The Life of Jesus series (almost 150 paintings by the Florentine Giovanni del Cinque [1667–1743]), two pictures by Lucca Giordano,

the Fall on the Road to Calvary by Mengs, and the famous Hunting Horn by Velázquez.

But in the personal view of this author, these important canvases should be added: the series The Works of Charity by Luis Ferrant (1806–1868); the portrait of Infanta María Antonia Victoria, la "Marianina," who was queen of Portugal, by Sani; and a Saint Vincent de Paul by Vicente López (1772–1850).

Twenty-eight limestone putti embellish the main stairway, made by the French sculptors Hubert Dumandré (1701–1781) and André Bertrand (d. 1772). The fine work of Dumandré is readily noticeable on the right side of the stairs, while the somewhat less refined pieces of Bertrand are on the left.

The most spectacular sculpture made for Riofrío is the altarpiece for the palace chapel by Dumandré begun in 1758 in his Balsaín workshop. The sculpture is made of white Borba marble from the Portuguese quarries near the Bragança palace in Villa Viçosa and of Spanish marbles, from Cabra, Espejón, and Mañaria.

Dumandré's altarpiece is no longer in Riofrío. It was moved in 1782 to the Cathedral of Segovia by permission of King Carlos III. The design to adapt it to the back of the cathedral choir is the work of the architect Ventura Rodríguez. An altarpiece created more than two hundred years ago for a palace chapel with an elliptical floor plan was so wisely adapted to a Gothic cathedral that one would pray for it to remain there.

Only some of the best works of the Riofrío collections have been mentioned. As important as the collections themselves are, the architecture that houses them is the most faithful and least altered of all Spanish royal palaces now extant.

There is a final note about Riofrío and its gardens that never were. The architect Virgilio Rabaglio had a garden in mind, probably on the west, north, and east sides of the palace. After he was unjustly fired from the project, subsequent changes ruled out his idea of a garden filled with fountains. Rabaglio was also an engineer, and had considered building a dam in the Peces River as well as hydraulic installations to supply water to a garden. One more loss, taken from the Palace of Riofrío by the wind of history.

REALES ALCÁZARES de SEVILLA

✣

REALES ALCÁZARES de SEVILLA

✠

The Roman Hispalis was one league south of Italica and more than two leagues south of the historic ford of Alcalá, across the Guadalquivir and near the bank, before arriving at the necropolis. Some writers say that the site of the later palace was in the praetorium itself and others that it was at the far end of the open area, next to the forum. Like any palace location, this site was carefully chosen and because of its Roman beginnings the Reales Alcázares de Sevilla is the oldest Spanish, or even European, palace that, along with La Almudaina in Palma, remains a royal residence and center of power.

With somewhat more precision, we know that in Visigothic times, a basilica stood on this site, dedicated to Saint Vincent according to some writers, but this was clearly a Christian necropolis. It later became a mosque, from the time of the Muslim invasion in the eighth century until the Normans sacked the area in 844. Again, it was the magic of the place that moved the rulers and architects of Islamic Sevilla to restore the original building after the Norman invasion. A Syrian, Abdallah-ben-Sinan, took the job under the caliph Abd-al-Rahman II (reigned 822–852), and this reconstruction resulted in a rectangular walled and turreted fortress, with a court of honor that more or less coincides with the present Flag Courtyard. That was the core of the early alcazar, the Dar-al-Imara, or Governor's House. It was the residence of the deputies in Sevilla of the three caliphs of Córdoba from the tenth century Ommeya dynasty: Abd-al-Rahman III al-Nassir the Great, his son Al Hakam II, and his grandson Hisham II.

Dar-al-Imara was absorbed by the southward growth of the city, as the building itself grew to the west toward the Guadalquivir River, to link with the eighth-century harbor fort. Ties with Córdoba were cut about 1030, and when the last caliph, Hisham III, died in 1036,

Sevilla became an independent kingdom. At that time the fortified complex was called Al-Ksar-al-Mubarak, the palace of the blessed or fortunate one. The residential area of the palace was then in the southwest section of the present complex, with the original Dar-al-Imara at one side in approximately the present location of the Patio de Carlos V. This would explain the position of the main entrance in the north wall, a modest horseshoe arch framed by a simple post and lintel under a bearing arch. The walls of the rooms, halls, and gardens of the new Al-Mubarak palace reflected the brilliant poetic vein of the poet king Al-Mutamid, who took his verses with him to exile and dreamed until his death of returning to his beloved Sevilla.

The Almoravide invaders plundered and ruined most of the Al-Mubarak, which shifted the center of power to the east during the splendid Almohade era that followed. Almost at the same time as the reconstruction of the fortifications and the river shipyards, the Torre del Oro (Tower of Gold) was erected and a pontoon bridge built across the river to Triana. Later, a great new mosque was constructed, and its minaret (La Giralda Tower of the Christian cathedral) became the symbol and banner of the city as well as one of the most beautiful towers in the world.

The Almohade rehabilitation of Dar-al-Imara must have centered on a new two-level garden, which was strengthened again in the eighteenth century, particularly in the Patio de Yeso (Gypsum Courtyard) area. Little is left of the Almohade civil architecture. Aside from its undeniable beauty, the Patio de Yeso has the value of a rare remain, although it also had an influence on the Alhambra of Granada. The Patio de Yeso shows how an extreme economy of materials can achieve maximum beauty—a sheer curtain of stone lace, with three arches at either side of a central arch. Through these one can see the wall behind, with a double-horseshoe arch in the middle, trimmed by a very fine frame. Despite its fragility, this work has survived for a thousand years. Perhaps centuries of neglect enshrouded the fretwork and saved it until it was uncovered in the nineteenth century and restored in the twentieth.

During the twelfth and thirteenth centuries the Almohades made Sevilla the capital of their Maghreb empire. In the last Almohade phase of less than a hundred years, the Mu'nimid dynasty added new defenses at the south of the palace complex, enclosed by a wall that surrounded the orchards and gardens of the alcazar. In the last third of the twelfth century king Abu-Yakub-Yusuf and his son king Yakub al-Mansur built their own palace at the south of the Almohade core where the Patio de Yeso is located. This new building had a handsome crossover courtyard similar to the Al-Mubarak courtyard that was protected from the sun by the palace. In time the Mu'nimid palace and garden became Christian and were known as the Gothic Palace and the Patio de María Padilla. In 1212 the allied Christian armies led by Alfonso VIII of Castilla defeated Muhammad al-Nassir, son of King al-Mansur in the battle of Las Navas de Tolosa; and by mid-century the Castilians reached the upper course of the Guadalquivir River (Wad-el-Kebir, in Arabic), seriously threatening the main Muslim centers of Córdoba and Sevilla. Fernando III (1202–1252), king of Castilla and León, grandson of Alfonso VIII, captured Córdoba in 1236 and the long-desired Sevilla in 1248.

Sevilla was now in Christian hands, the Almohade Umar-al-Murtada, grandson of the great Emir Yusuf I was a vassal of Castilla and León, and King Fernando resided in the alcazars! For the Sevillian fortress, this event was as important as the collapse of the Visigothic kingdom five centuries earlier. Fernando III was charmed by Andalucía and became a Sevillian. Continuing to advance south, he took Jerez and Cádiz, and died in the Sevillian Alcázares in 1252 at the age of fifty. If one result of his conquest, or reconquest—including Baeza, Andújar, Jaén, Córdoba, and other cities—was the expulsion of the Muslims from their homes and lands, the effects on the Sevillian alcazars were even more far-reaching. A new architectural language of great symbolic meaning was overlaid in the service of the new power.

Alfonso X (1221–1284), Alfonso the Wise, son of Fernando III, considered Sevilla so important that he made it the capital of his kingdom. Professor Fernando Chueca explains the phenomenon precisely: "It was the Wise king who built the Gothic Palace inside the Sevillian Alcazar, continuing a reaction that can be observed after the conquest. A sort of Cistercian version of the northern architecture was introduced in both Córdoba and Sevilla. . . . In Sevilla, the church of Santa Ana de Triana and the new Gothic Palace are representative of such a reaction . . . nevertheless, in the long run, the architecture of Islamic roots prevailed, with its seductive accents and its special brilliance."

Professor Rafael Manzano Martos, of the University of Sevilla, points out an interesting aspect of this Andalusian crossbreeding with the Gothic: "The Cistercian plainness and absence of decoration followed the ascetic teachings of Saint Bernard, in the same manner as Almohade art was a consequence of the severe diatribes of Ibn Tumart against the decorative excesses of the Almoravide mosques." Manzano is right in mentioning Muhammad Ben Tumart, a zealous twelfth-century leader from southern Morocco, in connection with the restrained Cistercian and Almohade styles that were combined as the basis of the Sevillian Mudejar, inspired in the Toledan Mudejar and with the Nazarite perfume of Granada.

Alfonso X's palace was designed in the elemental, metamorphic Gothic style and built on the almost one-hundred-year-old palace of the great Almohade kings. Medieval sources call this Christian palace the "Sea Shell Square" because of the spiral stairways in the turreted corners of its rectangular plan. Again it follows the familiar donjon scheme similar to the Mallorcan Almudaina, although with a different functional arrangement. The Sevillian palace had two elongated rooms side by side lengthwise, one looking south to Yusuf's Almohade gardens and the other north to the crossover garden of the same period. Both rooms connected at their east and west ends to other smaller rectangular rooms. Alfonso X gave cultural glitter to the great Christian cities, Toledo, a veritable emporium of literature and science, and Sevilla, where the poetic vein of King Al-Mutamid still throbs and where King Alfonso was inspired to compose his ballad, the "Cantigas de Santa Maria."

Certain historic events in southern Andalucía by mid-fourteenth century led to the enlargement and completion of the Sevillian palace. Alfonso XI (1312–1350), Alfonso the Righteous, secured the Strait of Gibraltar for the Christians to prevent Muslim penetration from North Africa and keep the Nazarite kingdom of Granada isolated. Yusuf I of Granada, allied with the Beni-Merins took Gibraltar and Tarifa. This was a mistake because it provoked an immediate Christian reaction and a Portuguese, Castilian, and Catalan allied army under Alfonso XI defeated the Granadans and Beni-Merins at the battle of the Salado River in 1340. With the booty that was captured, the Castilian king was able to undertake several campaigns using Genoese mercenaries. He also decided to build two royal houses. One of these was in the far north, in the city of Tordesillas on a hill over the Douro River. The building is a true gem of Mudejar secular art. It soon became a convent and still is today after seven centuries.

The second royal building was in Sevilla, where Alfonso ordered a Sala de Justicia (Hall of Justice) built in its Alcázar. The hall is an oblong room of relatively modest size in plan, 10 by 12 meters, but generous in height. It had a direct entrance through the Alcázar access courtyard (currently named the Patio del León, the Courtyard of the Lion), plaster niches in the Toledo style on the side walls, an octagonally coffered ceiling, and an east opening to the charming old Patio del Yeso. The Sala de Justicia demonstrates the eruption of the Mudejar style in alcazars. The location was certainly well chosen, and the room emerged as an Islamic *qubba* (poet's hall) under the carved and coffered ceiling. Pedro I, Alfonso XI's son, consecrated this hall forever with the blood of his stepbrother Don Fadrique, grand master of Santiago, whom he ordered stabbed to death there.

But the great work of Pedro I (1334–1369), called Pedro the Cruel by the nobles and Pedro the Righteous by commoners, was the new Mudejar palace on the old Al-Mubarak structures, at the southwest corner of the enclosure. Professor Ana Marín Hidalgo, an expert on this palace, states that "the construction was completed from 1364 to 1366 by masons and carpenters of Muslim origin, some Sevillian and others from Toledo and Granada." Indeed, Pedro I asked his ally Muhammad V of Granada to send him artists who could reproduce the marvels of the Nazarite palace. But the building, continued later by the Trastámara dynasty, contained not only Nazarite motifs but also caliphal, Toledan, and Almohade elements. As always, it was a crucible for blending the most diverse ingredients into a new architecture erected on an old foundation, not so much for the pleasure of destroying but with a constant wish to renovate and resurrect.

Taking advantage of the venerable *qubba* and altering the old alignment of the Al-Mubarak palaces, a new building was erected on an east-west axis around a pleasantly scaled central courtyard, 21 by 15 meters, surrounded by very beautiful arcades and abutting the westside room of Alfonso X's Gothic Palace, the room he used as a chapel. Looking on the main courtyard, the Patio de las Doncellas (Courtyard of the Maidens) are three rooms, two of them rectangular and opposite one another. The room to the north is El Dormitorio de los Reyes Moros (The Bedroom of the Moorish Kings), in reality the bedroom of the Christian kings. The room to the south, the Salón de Carlos V, has a formidable coffered vault, thus it is also known as the Hall of the Barrel Arch. The third room, at the west side of the courtyard, is the Salón de Embajadores (Hall of the Ambassadors), and it is the building's central element. With an almost square floor plan and a hemispheric dome—the celestial vault again—it is a richly decorated space, penetrated by adjacent areas through the play of three horseshoe arches on three sides, while the fourth side is open to the courtyard. Pedro I respected the basic skeleton of the *qubba* in introducing this room, but he was only able to begin the construction. The dome was not closed until the fifteenth century, and in the sixteenth century some alterations and new construction were still in process. Don Pedro's palace is complicated to describe, but it is even more difficult to convey the feeling it gives the visitor. Architecture rarely is so moving. The silent walls and corridors, the sudden beams of light, the intricate spaces of the Sevillian Alcázar constantly stimulate and surprise, each touching the curious mind and spirit differently. One might think the building happened by anarchical fits and starts, but it has been thought out with infinite care. Yet instead of using excessive weight, overwhelming volumes, and hard edges, it impresses only by suggestion, subtlety, and closure using only plaster, colors, and aromas. A closed and veiled architecture that is also open, intimate, and fleeting, pure contradiction that can only be understood by experiencing it. Coherence is unnecessary in this array of cultural influences crowded into a single place that is both changing and permanent. In this palace, Don Pedro took his leave of María de Padilla, his lover, to meet his death at the hands of his stepbrother in Montiel. According to legend Pedro said goodbye to María, "Leaving her under the roses and orange blossoms, on the other side of spring."

Thus a complex and marvelous palace was ready to live its happiest history under the banners of Christianity, after emerging from a five-century-old Islamic dream. In the fifteenth century, in the Lower Hall of the Alcázar, prince Juan was born, the issue of King Fernando and Queen Isabel on whom so much hope was placed and whose death in Salamanca at nineteen changed happiness into deep frustration. In this Alcázar his mother prayed, reading her Book of Hours; and in the old Al-Mutamid palaces she founded the Casa de Contratación, a clearing house for sailors and merchants. *La Virgen de los Mareantes* (The Seafarers' Virgin) hangs in its restored chapter hall, the best painting by the Sevillian artist Alejo Fernández (c. 1475–1546). Christopher Columbus was received in these halls on his return from his second trip to the West Indies. Other grand maritime expeditions to the New World were planned here, including the charting of Magellan's attempt to sail around the world in 1519.

The wedding of Emperor Carlos V (King Carlos I of Spain) to the Princess Isabel of Portugal in the Alcázar in spring 1526 was a splendid celebration attended by many renowned figures in the Hall of the Ambassadors. In keeping with the poetic tradition of Al-Mutamid, two of the best writers of the Renaissance were honored guests, Garcilaso de la Vega (1503?–1536), captain of the king's armies and one of the great Spanish poets, and Baldassare de Castiglione (478–1529), the papal nuncio and author of *The Courtier*.

Felipe II too, visited the Reales Alcázares, in May 1570, possibly in response to a problem with the Moors. About fifty years later, a young Scottish prince, then twenty years old, was a guest in the Alcázares of another Spanish king, who was himself not yet twenty. That summer of 1623 they talked about a Sevillian painter of almost the same age. An excellent portraitist, the painter had done "a quick sketch of the prince who paid him one hundred escudos." The prince asked to bring the painter to his kingdom, but he failed. The prince wanted to marry the Spanish king's sister, Doña María, and he failed. The offer to the artist failed because he wanted to remain in Spain and serve his king. And the political future of the unfortunate prince also failed when he was beheaded later in Whitehall. The prince was King Charles II of England, the painter Velázquez, and the Spanish king Felipe IV.

The Sevillian Reales Alcázares also shone under the Bourbon dynasty. Felipe V lived in the palace for almost five years, and his queen Isabel de Farnesio gave birth there to their last daughter, the Infanta María Antonia Fernanda, who became queen of Sardinia. The Lisbon earthquake in 1755 affected in varying degrees many historic buildings in western Spain. The brick and plaster of the Reales Alcázares were shaken, and the engineer Sebastian van der Borcht (active in Sevilla, mid-eighteenth century) was engaged to carry out the restoration. His excellent overall floor plan in color, dated April 10, 1759, throws considerable light on the Alcázar at that time. The earthquake had damaged the split-level Almohade garden so seriously that its lower level had to be filled in, which caused important changes in the garden and its surroundings.

Van der Borcht's plan indicates in red the existing parts of the building and in yellow the parts that were to be rebuilt. The document is very interesting as a graphic record of the eighteenth-century palace. The Almohade palace was made into a maze of partitions and rooms that rendered it unrecognizable. The Patio del Yeso was no more; it had been divided into the Clerk's Office, the Physician's Office, and the War Treasurer's Office. Similarly, the west area, the old palace of Al-Mutamid, was filled with spurious, worthless construction. The engineer must have had to work strenuously throughout most of the complex. This was especially true of the Gothic Palace of Alfonso X, to which he added a Bath Gallery open to the Patio de María de Padilla, "where a mezzanine is being built that will be suitable in its strength and height for housing the Royal retinue, connected to the main dining room and the Royal Chapel, and now will be useful for the Academy of Letters, which has no place for the winter, nor does the library or the curios collection whose entrance may be through the Tribune of the same hall, and this is desirable as a building gains nothing if it is not inhabited." Surely the governors and aides of the

Enlightenment, like Francisco Bruna and Pablo de Olavide, were grateful to Van der Borcht for his renovations and above all for his good will.

In the title block of Van der Borcht's drawing is a 70-Castilian-yard scale, its metric equivalent approximately 1:370. His measurements and angles are extraordinarily accurate, a difficult feat in a building where the orthogonal is conspicuously absent. The drawing is also admirable in its coloring, its notes, and its faithful reproduction of the gardens, and it includes the pavilion of Carlos I built by the Jew Juan Hernández in 1545 on an old Almohade *qubba*. An element that was designed but never built is a huge rectangular building east of the large pond, today the Pond of Mercury. The building was 50 by 40 meters in plan, with a central courtyard and at least two storys. While its purpose is not known, its clean, right-angled geometry would have been a rationalist blow to the present Murillo Gardens. Professor Manzano, who has been curator of the Alcázar for many years, characterizes the projected building: "Some more lines of script, this time ordered and aligned, in the millennium-old palimpsest of the Sevillian Alcázares."

Negligence and incompetence harmed the palace in the first half of the nineteenth century, but this was exceeded in the second half of the century by the actions of followers of the Romantic movement. Dubious construction in the Patio de las Muñecas (Courtyard of the Dolls) was aligned on a north-south axis with the Hall of the Ambassadors and joined the east-west axis of the Hall of the Ladies-Ambassadors. The palace was redecorated to house the Queen Mother Isabel II who traveled to Spain from her Paris exile in the Palace of Castilla near L'Etoile, where she had lived for more than nine years. She came for the wedding of her son King Alfonso XII, in Madrid, in January 1878, passing through Santander and El Escorial with her daughters, the infantas Pilar, Paz, and Eulalia. The party stayed in

Madrid only long enough to attend the marriage ceremonies, since the government had ordered her to leave the capital and reside in Sevilla. Eulalia, then thirteen years old, recalled later, "We were to go to Sevilla for the winter, where the Moorish Alcázar was being prepared to receive Isabel II and her entourage." The stay was shorter than anticipated because Isabel II was uncomfortable living close to the Sevillian Palace of San Telmo, where her estranged sister Luisa Fernanda and her sister's husband, the duke of Montpensier, held a kind of second court.

In the first third of the twentieth century Alfonso XIII and his wife, Ena of Battenberg, also stayed in the Reales Alcázares when they visited Sevilla. During these years the gardens were enlarged, and the exceptional Marchena Gate was added to enrich the gardens, purchased personally by the king from the estate auction of the Duchy of Osuna.

Three recent events should be mentioned. The first is the visit of Queen Elizabeth II of Great Britain to Spain in October 1988. Sevilla received her warmly, and she was lodged in the Alcázares. With the king and queen of Spain, she attended a *flamenco* performance in one of the palace courtyards. This was the first official visit of a British sovereign to Sevilla.

The second event, in 1992, was the Quincentennial of the Discovery of America. Spain celebrated the event with the Olympic Games in Barcelona and the Exposición Universal in Sevilla. The Spanish royal family visited the exhibition often during its six-month run. They stayed in a wing on the east side of the Reales Alcázares, above the seventeenth century pied-à-terre built by Vermondo Resta (c. 1550–1625). This space was adapted by the architect Manuel del Río and inaugurated in 1991 as a royal residence.

The third event was the wedding of the infanta Elena in March 1995. The Reales Alcázares, a stage for the pageantries of Muslim and Christian monarchs, renewed their enduring identity.

✣

The PALACE of LA ALMUDAINA,
PALMA de MALLORCA

✣

The PALACE *of* LA ALMUDAINA, PALMA *de* MALLORCA

✠

La Almudaina in Palma de Mallorca and the Reales Alcázares in Sevilla are the oldest buildings of the Spanish Crown. They form a unique pair, different from the Renaissance or Baroque palaces in their antiquity, their particular nature, and their dynamics of growth.

A study of these millennial buildings requires an unconventional methodology. Clearly, the anatomy and physiology of La Almudaina's architecture are closer to the biological rhythms of long aggregation and adaptation than to the conventional architectural criteria of modern times. La Almudaina's soul, its nature, and its reason for being lie in this uniqueness.

John Ruskin once remarked that "the greatest glory of a building is its age." His Romantic statement applies here in that the matter and substance of the Palma palace is more time and history, testimony and permanence, than walls, vaults, ogives, or crenellations. Its lively and changing character, its varied and multiform appearance, far from revealing an exact, unalterable origin, faithfully reflect the Mediterranean soul—that junction of many roads and cultures. The Mediterranean world has been a tapestry woven by the commercial and warring itineraries of Rome, Carthage, Greece, and Phoenicia in ancient times, and by Byzantium, Genoa, Aragón, and the Ottoman Empire in the Middle Ages. It is, therefore, not strange to think that the present cosmopolitan and touristic aspects of Mallorca are just one more step on the long, winding, picturesque stairway of the Balearic soul. In this sense, La Almudaina would be the most visible sign of this evolution. And the most intimate core of the palace would not be only the earliest architectural skeleton, or the deepest Roman or megalithic foundations, but rather that intangible spirit that has animated the Castell Reial (Royal Castle, in Mallorcan) from its inception.

An evocation of history is required to turn back two thousand years and see the arc of the Bay of Palma from the ocean. At the foot of the old *riera* (river), which has now been detoured to make a lively promenade, a broad hillock dominated the river and the bay, the natural strategic point for a defensive structure and a lookout. The hillock dropped sharply on the river side and sloped more gently toward the shore of the bay, facilitating access by ship from the shore to the southwest wall.

We can only guess at the architectural shape of the first structures in the Talayot (watchtower, in Mallorcan) of pre-Roman times. A survey of its foundations surely will throw some light on this historic area under the layers of two millennia. We know for certain, however, that the Carthaginians and the Romans, whatever their residential or bellicose intentions, maintained the privileged site chosen by its first builders. It is safe to think of this site as the generator of the city of Palma that grew around it in about the year 1,000, shaped first by the Carthaginian and Roman cultures and later by the Visigothic in the fifth and sixth centuries.

There is more historical data on this fortified nucleus from the relatively more recent Muslim invasion and from viewing its construction forms. It was transformed into an *almudaina,* or citadel, the Medinat-Mayurca, that was a stronghold for defending the bay and island as well as a residence-alcazar for the Muslim prince. Then, in about the tenth and eleventh centuries, it may have been an aloof *kasbah* (*alcazaba,* in Spanish) of sunlit sedimentary limestone walls with small windows and loopholes.

The building would have been a rectangle with towers in the corners, its longer side parallel to the shoreline, and with a fifth tower inserted between the two in the back, or northwest, facade. This fortress would also have had a turreted first enclosure at the higher level of the hillock, complemented later by a second enclosure at the lower river level, to protect the access from this side. The layout of the second enclosure created an opening directly on the bay side of the fortress, where the large Arco del Espalmador was built. Its graceful shape makes it one of the most singular arches in the island. The perimeter of the first enclosure probably coincided with the present building. The second, lower wall might have enclosed the gardens known today as the Hort del rei (King's Orchard). The main section of the Islamic castle was its five-towered alcazar, perhaps in the manner of the early medieval donjon.

A major transformation occurred in the thirteenth century when the Christians under Jaime I of Aragón (1208–78) conquered the Balearic Islands, from 1229 to 1235. Overlaying more than five centuries of Muslim culture with many new structures, they made La Almudaina a *castell* (castle). But this growth was not anarchical, inasmuch as the additions fulfilled functional requirements and were integrated with the whole. On the southeast side, facing the sea and physically attached to the old alcazar, the Grand Hall, or *Tinell*, was built, with a floor added to the original core. The main entrance to the walled enclosure was open on the west side; and its unroofed interior space was gradually reduced by adding new structures adjoining the walls on both the east and north sides. A powerful structure was erected on the west, perpendicular to the shoreline of the bay and leaning on the ramparts, the so-called Palau des Dones (Ladies' Palace) to lodge the Christian queens. Finally, almost in the center of the original enclosure, the chapel of Santa Ana was built, connected to the Christian palace by its gable end. An important, indeed inevitable, part of a Spanish palace, the chapel altered the volumes of the simple fortification scheme. At the same time, it undoubtedly added an aesthetic richness to the complex.

By juxtaposing new constructions to earlier ones, a palace plan was being formed that is very similar to what exists today. A wide front facing the bay was formed by the alcazar (already a royal palace) and the Grand Hall; and the queen's palace was a long, thick-walled structure with three projections, La Recambra (The Bedroom),

de la Regina (The Queen's Dressing Room), and de les Dones (Ladies' Room). The heavy walls continue up to the northwest corner where the Torre del Caps (Tower of the Heads) is situated. The tower was restored in the early twentieth century in an exaggerated interpretation of the Romantic ideal. The Torre del Celler (Warehouse Tower) was in the northeast corner, so named because it housed the royal storeroom and wine cellar. Another stretch of wall continued from that point, with another tower, La Squella (The Bell), in the center. The wall faced the *prat* (meadow) where the new *Seo* (Cathedral) was erected, and then continued on to the southwest tower that closed the perimeter.

In the center of the walled enclosure, the Chapel of Santa Ana created four surrounding courtyards: the Honor Courtyard to the east; the little El Baño (The Bath) courtyard next to the fifth tower; the Queen's, or El Brollador (The Fountain) courtyard at the west; and at the north, adjacent to the cisterns, the back or queen's garden. With time, this basic scheme underwent all sorts of alterations, renovations, and camouflages, but it is now cleaned up and its earlier appearance to a large extent has been restored. The addition of the chapel created a garden for the queen, a garden always placed to the north in the purest Spanish tradition.

From the fourteenth century a plot of land had been reserved for a great Gothic cathedral, and for the past five hundred years the cathedral that was built there has dominated the two-millennia-old Almudaina. Rubén Darío, the great Nicaraguan poet, described one of his arrivals in Palma as follows: "At dawn the land of Mallorca, the Island of Gold, was already visible. Then, the nearby islets were left aside . . . and the white ship entered the miracle of the bay of sweet Palma, whose cathedral, like an altar at sunset over the violet city, burns the sun like a flame."

This mother-daughter relationship between the cathedral and La Almudaina is hard to understand today considering that the fortress is, somehow, the mother of the cathedral. When the cathedral was built, the Almudaina was already over two thousand years old. If one mentally forgets the large volume of the cathedral and the play of light and shadow of its potent buttresses on the side facing the sea, the preeminent position of La Almudaina can be understood. With its Torre del Angel (Tower of the Angel), it was the grand lady of the bay. The cathedral itself, Darío's flame that set the sun afire, has burned La Almudaina for centuries.

Historical and archaeological research have increasingly validated Megalithic, pre-Roman, Carthaginian, and Roman construction. A stern Islamic Almudaina, the germ of the city growing around it, has also emerged with greater accuracy. From the thirteenth century onward, there is a Christian Almudaina, indebted to its Muslim past but filled with new Gothic buildings that erased or masked the mark of the Almoravides and Almohades. Jaime of Aragón and his son Jaime II ruled the independent Mallorcan kingdom from 1276 to 1311. His successors, Sancho, Jaime III, and Jaime IV, restored and ennobled La Almudaina as a Gothic royal residence. Its growing aesthetic value in the fourteenth and fifteenth centuries is well expressed in the palaces of the king and the queen. The Almudaina had become a Balearic acropolis.

The splendor of the Almudaina was darkened during the Renaissance of the sixteenth and seventeenth centuries. The architectural contributions of Gothic times were negated to some extent, particularly in the section oriented to the south—the alcazar and the Grand Hall. The severe, enclosed, alcazar had been embellished on the south and west with beautiful arches and ogives to soften the citadel aspect and adapt it to its new palace status. But from the sixteenth century onward, it was masked again with a number of galleries and closed facades that hid most of the medieval arches and ogives. The new defensive use of La Almudaina under Felipe II as well as an accumulation of functions assigned to the building later, reduced the palace to a state of aesthetic prostration. There were whimsical mutilations, additions, and fake superimpositions, made with questionable sensitivity and little respect for history.

José Vargas Ponce, a cultivated naval officer under Carlos III, charted the waters of the Mediterranean shore in the late eighteenth century. In his book *Descriptions of the Pithiusa and Balearic Islands* Vargas wrote:

The Palace of the General of the Island, where the Regent of the Law Court and the Quartermaster of the Realm also live, is a large

edifice with a poor layout and without order or taste; but its location facing the sea and the harbor, and its height which dominates a good part of the countryside, provide one of the most agreeable vistas imaginable. The complex comprises the Royal Chapel, the Law Court, Archives, Armory and a barracks for a Regiment of Cavalry; it has an ample garden, and within it, several fountains and a large pond.

A lithograph by Bichebois, dated in the first half of the nineteenth century, illustrates the mutilations of the once svelte Torre del Angel. Photographs taken in the 1860s and 1870s show very precisely not only the masked sixteenth-century galleries but also all sorts of walls, windows, roofs, and eaves, added crazily under the absurd dictates of petty needs. All of this converted the Almudaina into an immense, rambling building, ugly and intimidated by the great mass of the cathedral. In the last phase of its construction, about 1880, the cathedral acquired the brown limestone aspect that it now has.

In 1860 Queen Isabel's brief stay gave the Balearic Islands a long-desired royal visit, which brought about some ephemeral decorative touches to La Almudaina. But the September 1868 revolution that sent Isabel II into exile in Paris, led to the demolition of the monument to the queen that the city of Palma had erected eight years earlier. What has been termed the resurrection of La Almudaina began in a very timid way, at the end of the eighteenth century, thanks to the army engineers who undertook cleaning and reconstruction operations. This was followed by other reconstruction that was Romantic in inspiration, such as the rather exaggerated recreation of the Torre del Caps and above all the restoration of the Gothic chapel of Santa Ana. The enchanting Neo-Romantic style of the chapel's present facade relates to the theories of Viollet-le-Duc (1814–1879), a leading exponent of Gothic Revival architecture.

But the most important modifications of the building have taken place in the twentieth century. In the 1960s the east facade and the main gate were altered within the wider scope of rehabilitating the east and south wings to lodge General Franco, who was then head of state. These rooms were completed in 1967 but the general never used them, although thirty-four years earlier he was the military commander of the Balearic Islands and lived and worked in this building. The most felicitous and eloquent intervention occurred in the 1970s and 1980s, planned and directed by Manuel del Río. This involved restoring the centuries-old ogival vaults and the earlier profile of walls and towers, including bringing the Torre del Angel up to its initial height. The tower is the identifying sign of La Almudaina, and its crowning figure had been dislocated for the last two centuries. The Balearic flag, which displays the tower in silver on a violet field, again had meaning.

These new alterations are not the last, as there is still much to do on the Christian areas of Les Dones and San Jaime, but they have revived the secular use and name of La Almudaina: the royal palace. Each year the present monarchs, Don Juan Carlos and Doña Sofía hold official functions in the halls of the old Muslim alcazar (where both have their offices) and in the Gothic Tinell hall, where they receive the island authorities and grant audiences.

The upper floor of the alcazar core was modified in 1984 to make it a royal residence, as it was during the caliphs and kings of the Mallorcan kingdom. The royal couple spend the summer season in Mallorca, in a palace close to La Almudaina, named Marivent, which has superior communications facilities and is better adapted to modern living. But for protocol reasons, the Spanish monarchs often go to La Almudaina to perform official ceremonies, and they host their distinguished guests in the residential area of the alcazar. The city has an age-old spirit of hospitality and plurality, and it is indeed a crossroad for many cultures and peoples, represented in the stones, ogives, and crenellations of the old castle and royal palace of La Almudaina.

EPILOGUE

✠

Among this group of Spanish royal palaces, La Almudaina in Palma de Majorca and the Reales Alcázares in Sevilla, stand out because of their antiquity. As testimonials of history their status prevails over any conventional analytic methodology. La Almudaina has still another distinction: it belongs to the National Heritage of Spain, the public body entrusted with maintaining these royal residences. The Reales Alcázares are owned by the City of Sevilla, but through a special agreement signed in 1990 the monarchs may reside in this complex under the care of the National Heritage.

The other six palaces can be divided into a Renaissance group—Aranjuez, El Escorial, and El Pardo—and a Baroque group—La Granja, Riofrío, and Madrid, all with their adjacent pavilions. Each palace has its own origin, configuration, location, and current uses, which makes it difficult to assign common features, even from the merely functional standpoints of maintenance and conservation. This becomes even more complicated if one attempts to find common characteristics or develop general notions about the historic, aesthetic, or scientific character of these palaces. The great diversity of styles, historic periods, and personalities of the royalty and aristocracy, not to mention those of artists and craftsmen, has made scholars reserved and reflective when they are asked to identify a connective tissue, no matter how fragile, that unifies these buildings.

There is an answer, but it must be expressed with a certain caution and after prolonged debate. It can be summarized in four letters: R-O-M-E.

Rome indeed. Rome in its fullest sense. Rome the city and Rome the civilization. Republican Rome, Imperial Rome, Christian Rome, Renaissance Rome, Baroque Rome, and Papal Rome.

Rome hovers permanently over Spanish palaces, from simple philology to its influence on kings, aristocrats, and artists. A constant dream of the Roman Empire, passed on to Charlemagne and then to the Holy Roman Empire, to which Spain gave an illustrious emperor, César Carlos (Carlos V). But Rome is much more, she enters the lives of kings and artists with uncommon frequency and offers herself as a magnet, or at times as an inevitable, enchanting fetish. Without ancient Rome, the Empire, the Papacy, and the Roman Renaissance, Spanish palaces cannot be understood.

The word *palace* has its origin in the Palatine hill in Rome. It is where Cicero, Livy, and Augustus were born, and it was found recently that Augustus even painted some frescoes on his walls. The words *palais, palace, palacio, palast, palazzo,* and the modern name of the Dalmatian city of Split, the old *Spalato (es-palatium),* all derive from the imperial palace in the Palatinum, from which the Roman emperors could watch the races in the Circus Maximus. But this is more than a matter of etymology or phonetics. It is also semantic, because the implications of words are more profound than they might seem.

The Roman Empire recovered as an organizational aspiration from the time of Charlemagne and Otto I. The Holy Roman Empire, which lasted a thousand years, from Otto to Napoleon, was the mirror in which the princes of Europe looked at themselves and found the source of their authority and prestige. Napoleon, the creator of another empire, is portrayed in Roman dress on the victory column of the Place Vendôme.

As for the artists who worked during five centuries for the Spanish Crown, it may be argued that Mengs was a Bohemian, Mor a Dutchman, Sittow a Balt, Wall an Irishman, Michel, Frémin, Boutelou, and Dumandré French. But Italy was the great supplier of artists and artisans. Neapolitans, Venetians, Sicilians, Piedmonteses, and Savoyards passed through Rome, were educated in Rome, and owed their professional ability to Rome. Or else, they were Roman. Spanish palaces would not exist as such without Sacchetti, Juvarra, Sabbatini, Bonavia, Bernasconni, Titian, Tintoretto, Tiepolo, Panini, Bernini, Tacca, Rusca, Giaquinto, Ravaglio, and many others.

And the Spaniards? There was scarcely a Spanish artist of repute who did not spend time in Rome. Juan de Herrera was there as a soldier; Juan Bautista de Toledo worked in Saint Peter's as an assistant architect to Michelangelo under the name of Angelis; Villanueva studied in Rome for six years with a grant from the Academy. Velázquez would not be Velázquez without his two stays in Rome where he felt so at ease, learned so much, and met so many people. The same thing happened to the young Goya, whose obligatory passage through Rome transformed him. Procaccini and Subisati also came from Rome. And when artists themselves did not come from Rome, or from some part of Italy, they sent designs or their finished work from Italy. And what of the Milanese family Leoni? Leo, the father, remained in Milan; his son Pompeo came to the Escorial; and the grandson Michele became Miguel. Together the three left us some of the best sculptural groups of the Renaissance.

And the aristocrats? Scotti, Grimaldi, and Schilacci (Esquilache) came from Italy as well as many others who had a decisive influence on almost all of the royal buildings. Olivares, the favorite of Felipe IV, was Roman by birth. And finally, the kings. In this select group Rome and all of Italy have something to say. Spain has had seven Italian queens; Amedeo of Savoy was King of Spain; Carlos III was educated in Italy; and his son Carlos IV was Italian born and died in Rome. José I, usurper king of Spain, also died in Rome, as did Alfonso XIII, the grandfather of the present King Juan Carlos I, who was in turn born in Rome and baptized there by Cardinal Pacelli, later Pope Pius XII.

This text opens with a reference to the exhibition of Vatican treasures in New York authorized by Pope John Paul II, and it closes with a reflection on the papacy's contribution to Renaissance and Baroque Rome—to eternal Rome. Without the popes, the Rome of the arts would not be eternal. It would seem that antiquity has hidden forever in the city's ruins, erasing the grandeur of its past, and that only her powerful influence has remained in the souls of the kings and artists of the Spanish palaces.

One of the greatest writers in Spanish literature, Francisco de Quevedo, expressed the strength of Rome, both present and past, in this masterful sonnet, which in a free English version reads:

In Rome, pilgrim, you search for Rome,
and in Rome you will not find her:
proud walls are her cadaver
and her tomb the Aventine.

She lies where the Palatine reigned,
and the medals eroded by time,
show the ravages of ancient battles
obscuring the Latin insignias.

Only the Tiber remained, whose waters
washed the city, and now, sepulcher,
it weeps for her in doleful tones.

Oh, Rome!, In your greatness, in your beauty,
you fled what was solid, and now
only the fugitive endures.

✠

In this overview of the royal palaces of the Spanish Crown we have analyzed their origins, patterns of growth, and most significant losses along with the historical substratum that led to their creation and that has operated as the essential element in explaining why their architecture and decorative schemes are what they are.

Nevertheless, contrary to what a great contemporary Spanish poet expressed, with impertinence and irony, in one of his most celebrated poems,

Try not to look at its monuments,
traveler, if you are going to Rome . . .

many others urge us to look without caution, without cynicism but with curiosity, without arrogance but with intensified interest at those centuries-old royal palaces, temples of art, history, and life at its most courtly and most quotidian.

There could be no better complement to the preceding pages than an abundant selection of recent images of these royal palace complexes. Despite the passage of several centuries, many of the surroundings, arrangements, decorations, and colors are exactly the same as those seen and enjoyed by the kings, princes, and courtiers who lived in these palaces until a few years ago and were devoted to a continuity that is perpetuated today.

All of these palaces continue to be in full use, and they are the settings for official and cultural ceremonies of the Spanish Crown. Each day in their regal ambiances the ancient and beautiful designation "Royal Sites" is renewed.

Vista del rio con parte de Madrid y Real Palacio.

✠

The PALACE *of* MADRID

✠

93. *Panorama with the west side of the palace in the distance by the view painter Fernando Brambilla (1768–1832).*
Washerwomen at the Manzanares River in the foreground.
94–95. *The main or south façade toward the Plaza de la Armería.*
96. *The decorative ensemble of the vault above the main stairway. The central motif,*
Religion Protected by Spain, *by Corrado Giaquinto (1700–1765).*

97. Vault of the Salon of the Halberdiers. Venus Directing Vulcan to Forge the Arms of Aeneas
by Giovanni Battista Tiepolo (1696–1770).

The PALACE of MADRID
97

98. Detail of the armor of King Don Sebastião of Portugal, nephew of Felipe II.
99. Salon of the Halberdiers.

100. *Plus Ultra Buckler of Carlos V.*
101. *Salon of Columns. The ceremonies of the signing of the Treaty of Accession of Spain to the European Community in June 1985 and the opening of the Middle East Peace Conference in October 1991 were held here.*

102–3. Two ceiling frescoes by Giovanni Battista Tiepolo: Aeneas Receiving the Arms of Victory
from Venus in the Salon of the Halberdiers.
104. The Apotheosis of the Spanish Monarchy in the Throne Room.
105. The thrones of Don Juan Carlos and Doña Sofía in the Salón de Besamanos, known today as
the Throne Room, centered on the main palace facade looking south.

106–9. Ornamental details of the
Throne Room with crested mirrors
above the consoles.

110. Official antechamber. The round table in the center was a gift to Fernando VII from England.

111. Antechamber of Carlos III, with portraits of Carlos IV and María Luisa, by Francisco Goya (1746–1828).
112. The clock was made for the royal couple by Godon.
113. Detail of a console, first half of the 18th century.

The PALACE of MADRID

114. Official anteroom with consoles from the time of Carlos III.
The tapestries were made in the Royal Workshop after designs by Téniers.

115. Everyday Dining Room in the east wing.
116. Antechamber of Queen María Cristina de Habsburgo-Lorena with a portrait of Isabel de Farnesio.
117. Antechamber of Queen María Cristina.

118–19. Neo-Gothic chandeliers in the official chamber and the official antechamber.

120. *Antechamber of Carlos III decorated with paintings by Lucca Giordano (1632–1705).*

121. Details of the vault painting by Vicente López (1772–1850) in the Salon of Carlos III.
122–23. Vault fresco by Giovanni Battista Tiepolo in the Throne Room.

124. *Detail of the vault in the Salon of Mirrors with the Allegory of Painting by Francisco Bayeu (1734–1795).*

125. *Detail of the tapestry* Young David Praying, *in the Salon of Tapestries. 18th century.*
126. *Detail of the tapestry* Pentecost.
127. *Fragment of the tapestry* Marriage of David and Bathsheba. *16th century.*

The PALACE of MADRID

128. *Embroidered wall covering in the rare woods room of Queen María Luisa de Parma.*
129. *Embroidered border in blue tones made by the Royal Workshop in 1828 for the Salon of Carlos III.*
130. *Italian furniture flanked by a pair of harps made by Erard.*
131. *Painted wallpaper in the rooms of Infanta Isabel.*

132. Clock by Francisco Rivas.
133. Salon of Mirrors with china decorations made in the Buen Retiro Workshop.

134. *Details of the Salon Gasparini.*
135. *Chamber of Carlos III, or the Salon Gasparini, named for its Neapolitan designer Matteo Gasparini (d. 1774).*
136–37. *Details of the Salon Gasparini.*

138. *Detail of the Porcelain Room of Carlos III. The porcelain panels, console, and vases were made by the Buen Retiro Workshop. Console and vases are of the period of Carlos IV (reigned 1788–1808).*

139. *Salon of Tapestries.*

140. Gold-plated clock. Period of Isabel II, mid-19th century.
141. Clock by Jean-François de Belle (active Paris, 1781), with mechanical figures
representing Vulcan's forge. Salon of Carlos III.

142. Centerpiece, period of Fernando VII (reigned 1808–1833).

143. State Dining Room designed by José Segundo de Lema (d. 1891), commissioned by Alfonso XII in 1879.

144. Cabinet Meeting Room.
145. A room in the Royal Library in the style of Alfonso XII (reigned 1874–1885).
146. Detail and general view of the dome fresco of the Royal Chapel by Corrado Giaquinto.
147. View of the Royal Chapel.

148–49. West facade of the palace looking toward the Campo del Moro gardens and the fountain of the Tritons.

150. *Fountain of the Shells.*
151. *Fountain of the Shells at night with the east façade of the palace in the background.*

✠

The PALACE of EL PARDO

✠

153. *The Royal Site of El Pardo by Michel-Ange Houasse (1680–1730). In the Palace of Riofrío.*
154–55. *South facade of El Pardo. After the additions in the 18th century by Francesco Sabbatini it became the main facade.*
156–57. *Views of the west facade and bridge over the dry moat. This was the main facade from the time of*
Carlos I until the reign of Carlos III.

158. *Courtyard of the Austrias at El Pardo. The upper gallery reopened in 1988. The original balustrade, supported by inventive trun-*
cated arches and ornamental architraves, has few precedents in 16th century Spanish architecture.
159. *The famous Queen's Gallery on the north side of the palace.*
160. *Don Juan José de Austria, stepbrother of Carlos II, by José de Ribera, "El Españoleto" (1591?–1652), in the Queen's Gallery.*
161. *Detail of the gallery ceiling: Samuel from the Story of Joseph series, workshop of Eugenio Cajés (c. 1577–1634).*

·P·
SAMVEL

162. *Courtyard of the Bourbons. Glass roof covering built in March 1983 on the occasion of the 5th Centennial of El Pardo.*

164. Courtyard of the Bourbons. The glass roof allows its use as a reception room.
165. The 1988 restoration maintained the four corners that were chamfered in the 18th century.

166. *An ivory Virgin (1690) by Claudio Beissonet and an ivory crucifix (1589) by Gaspar Núñez Delgado*
(c. 1555–1606) in the private chapel of El Pardo.
167. Portrait of Isabel the Catholic by Juan de Flandes (fl. 1496–d.c. 1519) in the Official Salon.

168. *Detail of the table in Salon of Lyres.*
169. *Tapestry in the Trellis Galleries. Flanders. First quarter of 17th century.*
170. Hunting with Falcons *tapestry made in the Royal Workshop after a design by*
Guillermo Anglois (fl. second half of the 18th century).
171. *Meissen candelabra. 18th century.*

172. *Salon of Pompeiian Tapestries. Formerly the boudoir of Princess of Asturias María Luisa de Parma.*
173. *Vestibule of the Salon of the Ambassadors. Ceiling painting by Mariano Salvador Maella (1739–1819).*

174. *Official antechamber. Tapestries made by the Royal Workshop after designs by Zacarías González Velázquez (1763–1834).*

175. *Ceiling of the Official Salon, painted by Ramón Bayeu (1746–1794) in 1774,
with stucco reliefs by Robert Michel (1720–1786).*

The PALACE of EL PARDO

176–77. Two views of the Official Salon with tapestries representing The Battles of Archduke Alberto. *16th century.*
178. Theater of Carlos IV. North wing of the palace.

179. The Immaculate Conception *by Juan Bautista Peña (c. 1710–1773). Palace chapel.*

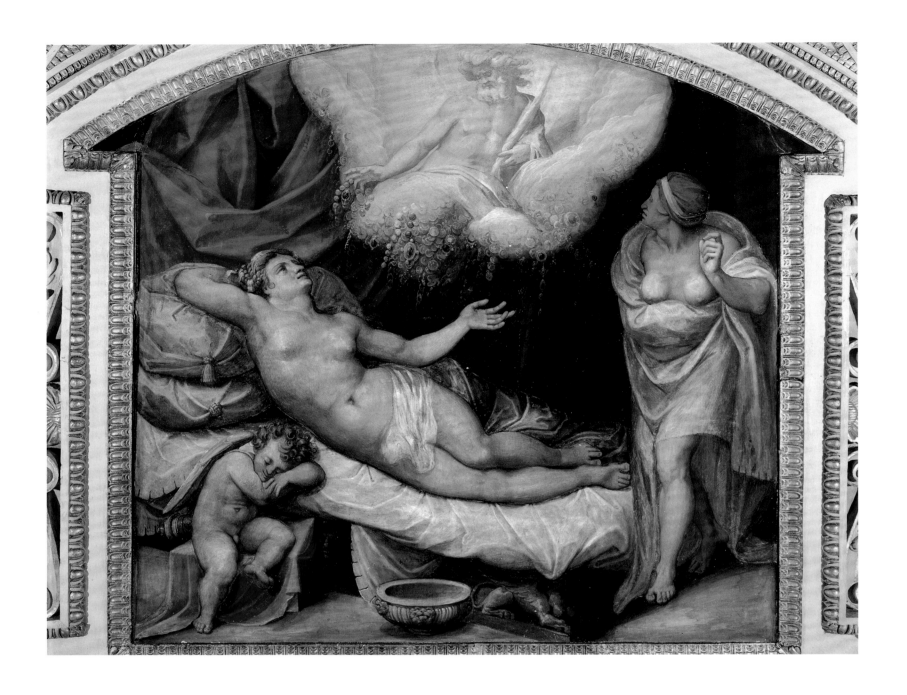

180. The Rain of Danae. *Fresco by Gaspar Becerra (1520?–1570). In El Torreón, the tower named for the artist.*
181. *Detail of tapestry* The Capture of the City of Hulst, *from the Battles of Archduke Alberto series.*
Woven by Martin Reybouts. Early 17th century. Official Salon.

182–83. Detail of frescoes by Juan Gálvez from the period of Fernando VII. Cabinet meeting room.
184. Tapestries from the Royal Workshop depict popular scenes based on designs by Goya, González Velázquez,
Aguirre, González-Ruiz, Bayeu, and Téllez. Cabinet Meeting Room.
185. Detail of clock on one of the consoles.

The PALACE of EL PARDO

186. *Tapestry with Chinese motifs designed by José del Castillo (1739–1793). Made by the Royal Workshop. Honor bedroom in El Pardo.*
187. *Piano Room. Screen painted by José María Sert (1874–1945).*
188. *Exterior view of the Palacete de la Quinta de El Pardo (country house).*

189. King Juan Carlos I, while still a prince, had his office in the Official Chamber of la Quinta de El Pardo.
Painted wallpaper with scenes of the conquest of Mexico. 19th century.
190–91. Detail of painted wallpaper. Official Chamber of La Quinta.

The PALACE of EL PARDO

192. *Painted wallpaper with flower garlands and draperies. 19th century. Audience Room. La Quinta.*
193. *Portrait of María Josefa Amalia de Sajonia, third wife of Fernando VII.*
194–95. *Audience Room. La Quinta.*

196. *Pompeiian sitting room. Casa del Príncipe (Prince's house). El Pardo. Embroidered silk decor made in the Lyons*
factory of Camilla Pernon by express request of the Prince of Asturias (later Carlos IV). Late 18th century.
197. *Dadoes and carved wood furniture, painted white and gilded.*
Made by the Royal Workshop. Late 18th century.

198. Salon of Stuccos in the Casa del Príncipe by Juan Bautista Ferroni (1741?–1806) in collaboration
with Esteban de Agreda and José Ginés.
199. View of the fountain and cascade of La Quinta. Beyond is the main building, restored in 1973.

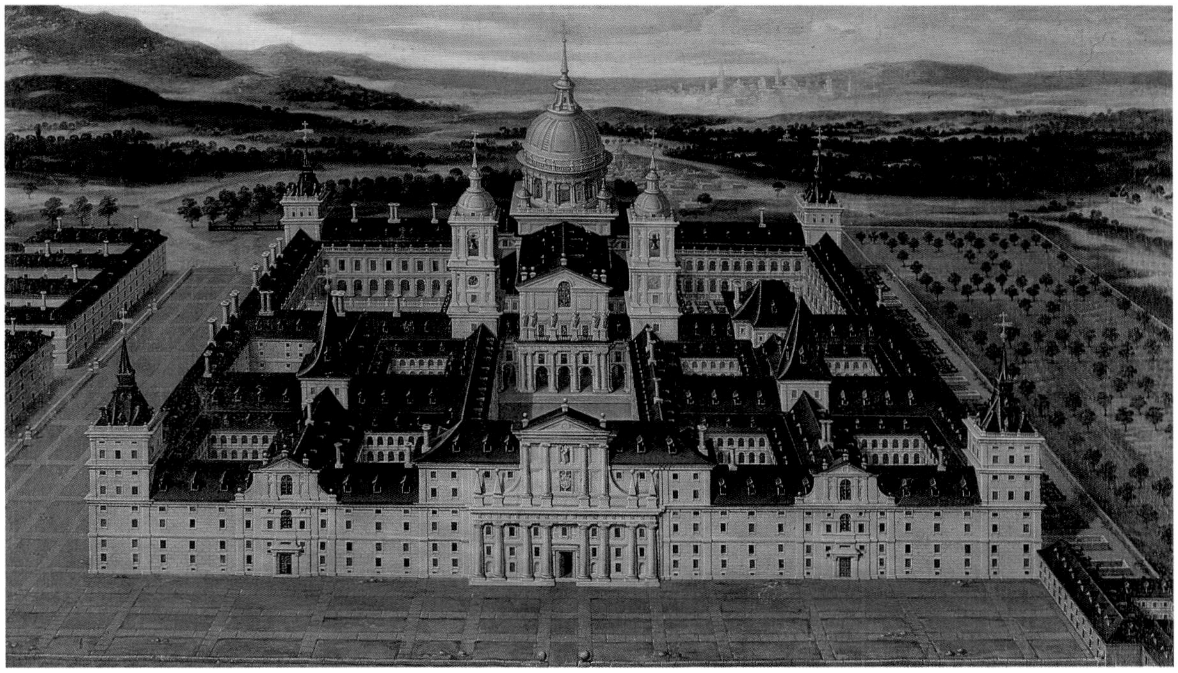

The PALACE *of* EL ESCORIAL

201. A projection from the west facade of El Escorial.
202. A night view of El Escorial from the Abantos mountain.
203. A perspective of the majestic front facade of El Escorial seen from a corner of the esplanade.

The PALACE of EL ESCORIAL

204. *The south facade of El Escorial.*

206. *The present garden with boxwood squares and La Herrería property in the background, an approximation of Felipe II's view four centuries ago from his private rooms.*
207. *Perspective of the south facade.*

208. *The famous pavilion designed by Juan de Hererra (c. 1530–1597) in the center of the Courtyard of the*
Evangelists, surrounded by four ponds and twelve boxwood squares. Originally designed as an
open gallery, it was closed in the 17th century with wood panels painted green.

209. *Upper cloister around the Courtyard of the Evangelists.*

210. *Altar of the Holy Sacrament in the sacristy of the basilica of El Escorial.*
211. *Carlos II's atonement resulted in the grand painting by Claudio Coello (1642–1693)*
Carlos II Worshipping the Holy Sacrament *(1690).*
212–13. *Details of* Carlos II Worshipping the Holy Sacrament.

214. Tapestry Los Paños de Oro (*The Golden Cloths*) *in the Hall of Honor.*
215. *Royal Gallery, often called the Hall of Battles.*
216–17. *Detail of the battle of La Higueruela.*

218. Portrait of Felipe II by
Antonio Moro (1519?–1576), a
wedding present from the king to his
second wife, Mary Tudor.

219. Clock-lamp by Haus de Evalo
for Felipe II.

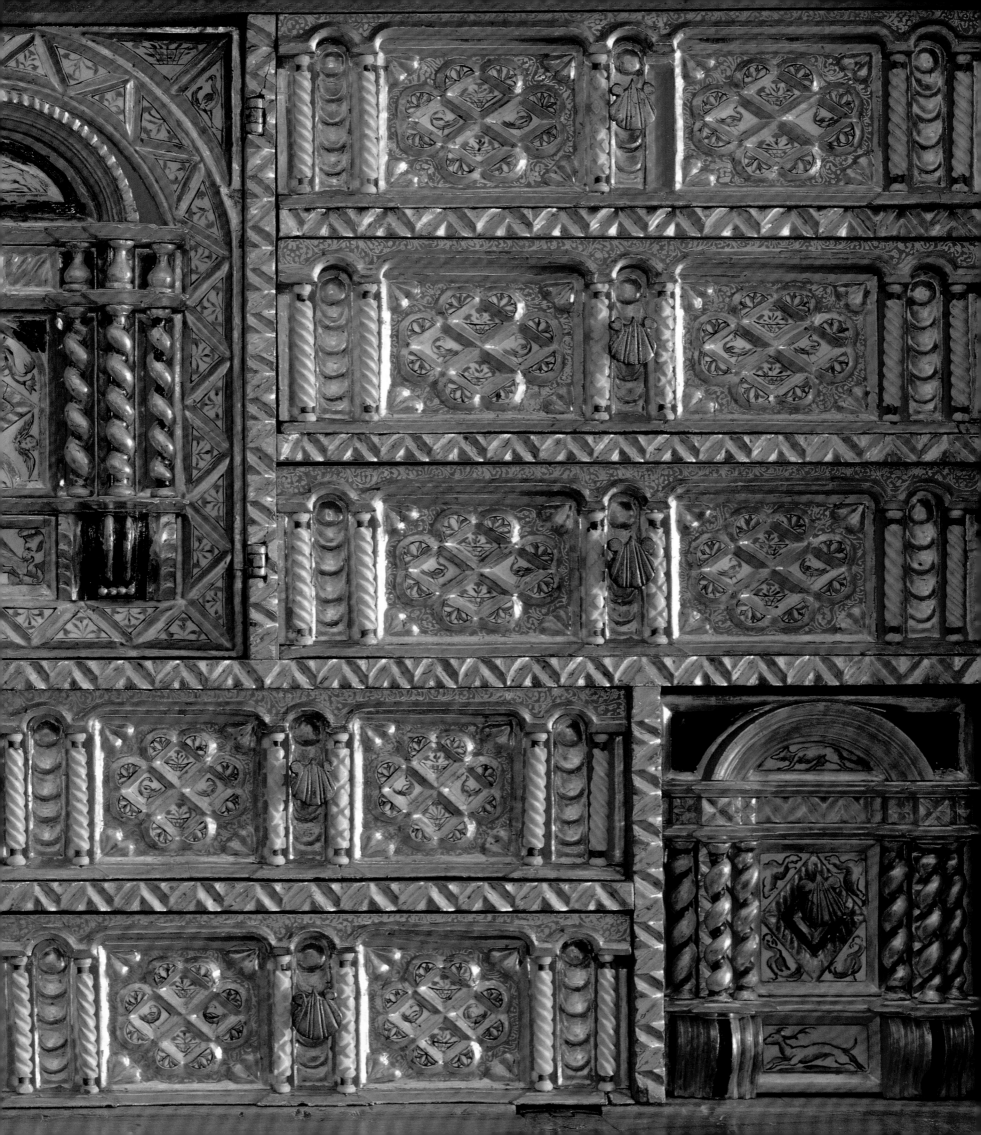

222. German door in the old
Salon of the Ambassadors in
the royal quarters of Felipe II.
223. View of the Royal
Gallery seen from the median
line inlaid in the floor during
the 18th century.

224. *Private rooms in the royal quarters of Felipe II.*
225. *Detail of the gilt-bronze portrait group by Pompeo Leoni (c. 1533–1608).*
Felipe II and his fourth wife, Ana de Austria.

226. *Pages from the Cantigas.*
227. *View of the Print Gallery in the Royal Library of El Escorial.*
228. *Detail from the Beatus of Liébana.*
229. *Flemish panel painting attributed to Vrancke van der Stockt in the large drawing room of Felipe II's quarters.*

manducauit ea fidentiu et audiui
uocem de celo dicentem scribe
Beati mortui qui in domino moriuntur

ndo habere non
pacatuf.
ihesum hic sit a que
agno copulatur
in magno labore in illa
ls coronetur
deuogationi aduersi
xpi prenati possi
faciat finem epistu
prequutagoru in asri
LIBER SEXTVS

SEPTIMVS:

um uolantem in medio
angelii basini ua
racunati in asri
ibu et lingua et pplo
in ciuitate et clari tate
nes et quodo quatei
asteru in asre sonef
gelus sendi sequutatis es
dia babilon illa
io fornicationis et
et angelus tertius

vbi angelus
ostendit euangelium
aeternum

230. The Haywain, *copy of the original by Hieronymus Bosch (c. 1450–1516) now in the Prado Museum.*
The copy hangs in the abbot's cell on the lower story at the southeast corner of the monastery.
231. *Detail of copy of* The Haywain.

232. *A fine copy of the Rogier Van der Weyden (1399?–1464)* Descent from the Cross *by Michel Coxcie (1499–1592).*
233. *Detail of copy of* Descent from the Cross.
234. Allegory of the Holy League *by El Greco (1541–1614). Probably painted for the tomb of Juan de Austria, who as victor at Lepanto is portrayed in the center foreground.*
235. *Detail of El Greco* Allegory of the Holy League.

236. *Detail of tapestry* The Roped Bull *designed by Francisco Bayeu (1734–1795). Royal Quarters of Carlos IV.*
237–38. *Salon of Ambassadors. Royal Quarters of Carlos IV.*

239. *Pompeiian-style tapestries designed by José del Castillo (1739–1793). Made by the Royal Workshop.*
Wet nurses' room in the Bourbon apartments.

240. *Main Hall of the Bourbon palace with tapestries designed by Francisco Bayeu.*

241. Anteroom, or first receiving room, of the Bourbon palace in El Escorial. Tapestries inspired by Flemish themes.
Made by the Royal Workshop.

242–43. Detail of the floor in one of the rooms "of rare woods."
244. Private office of Carlos IV, room "of rare woods." Northeast corner of the first floor.
245. Corner detail. Private office of Carlos IV.

246. Embroidery by Juan López de Robredo.
247. Set of embroideries made by Juan López de Robredo in 1797 for the Casita del Príncipe
(Prince's Little House) at El Escorial.

248–49. Two views of the Porcelain Room. Porcelains made by the Buen Retiro Royal Workshop
to imitate Wedgwood. Casita del Principe.
250. The former Red Hall, hung with paintings by Lucca Giordano (1632–1705). Casita del Principe.
251. Side room or Hunting Salon, with walls covered in yellow silk, Casa del Infante Don Gabriel.

252. Ceiling detail of the Salon Japelli in the Casita del Príncipe.
253. Vault with four oculi, probably painted by Vicente Gómez (d. 1792). In the central hall
of the Casa del Infante Don Gabriel.

254. *View of the Casita del Príncipe from the central pond.*
255. *View of the Casa del Infante Don Gabriel from the gardens.*
256. *View of the arbor of the Casa del Infante from the interior.*

257. *Aerial view of El Escorial from the southwest. At left the esplanade, La Lonja, with the Garden of the Friars in the foreground.*
258–59. *View of the college corner with Herrera's characteristic stone sphere on the parapet of the snow-covered esplanade.*

The PALACE of EL ESCORIAL

Vista de el R¹. Sitio de Aranjuez, de la Cascada grande y Palacio; tomada á la parte de Lebante.

✠

The PALACE of ARANJUEZ

✠

The PALACE of ARANJUEZ

264

261. East or back facade of the Royal Palace of Aranjuez, painted by Francisco Brambilla (1768–1832).
262–63. West or main facade seen from the Raso de la Estrella.
264. Northern tower viewed from the cascade known as "The Castanet."
265. View from the east.
266–67. Among the best-known fountains of the La Isla gardens are those of Apollo and Lo Spinario.

The PALACE of ARANJUEZ

268. Fountain of Apollo in the Prince's Garden.
269. Fountain of Apollo at the end of a tree-lined avenue.

270–71. *The play of light and water in the fountain of Ceres, in the garden at the west side of the palace.*

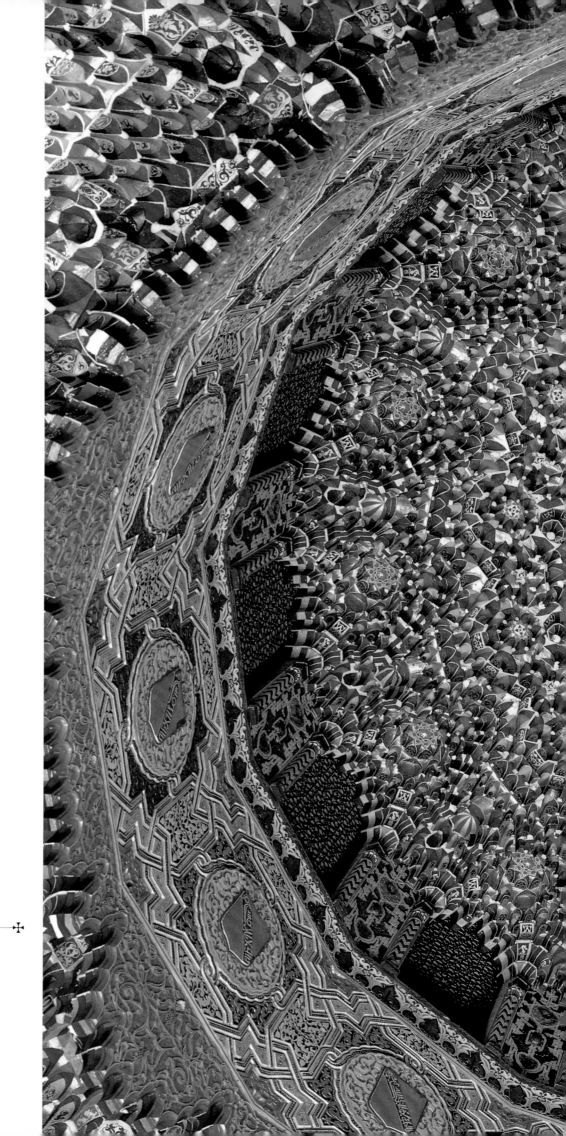

272. Detail of main stairway (1743–1746), by
Giacomo Bonavia (1705–1759) for Felipe V.
273. The Arab Room (1848–1850), designed by Rafael Contreras
(1824–1890) as a smoking room for King Don Francisco de Asís,
consort of Isabel II.
274–75. Ceiling detail. The Arab Room.

274

276. *Detail of the floor mosaic in the Sculpture Gallery. La Casita del Labrador.*

277. *Sculpture Gallery in La Casita. Designed by Jean-Demosthène Dugourc (1749–1825) with sculptures from the Villa Adriana. Side-wall niches were made for four sculptures by Antonio Canova, commissioned by Carlos IV but never executed. La Casita.*

278. Detail of the clock, made in France in 1800, in the Platinum Room. La Casita.
279. Corner of the Platinum Room, designed by Charles Percier (1764–1838) and Pierre Fontaine (1762–1853). La Casita.
280. Ceiling detail of the Platinum Room.
281. Porcelain Room. Floor and mirrors (1740–1745) by Giacomo Bonavia (1705–1759) for Felipe V. Carlos III ordered the
room finished by Neapolitan craftsmen with materials from the Capodimonte workshop in Naples.
The Caroline-style conversation room was completed in 1763. Palace of Aranjuez.

The PALACE of ARANJUEZ

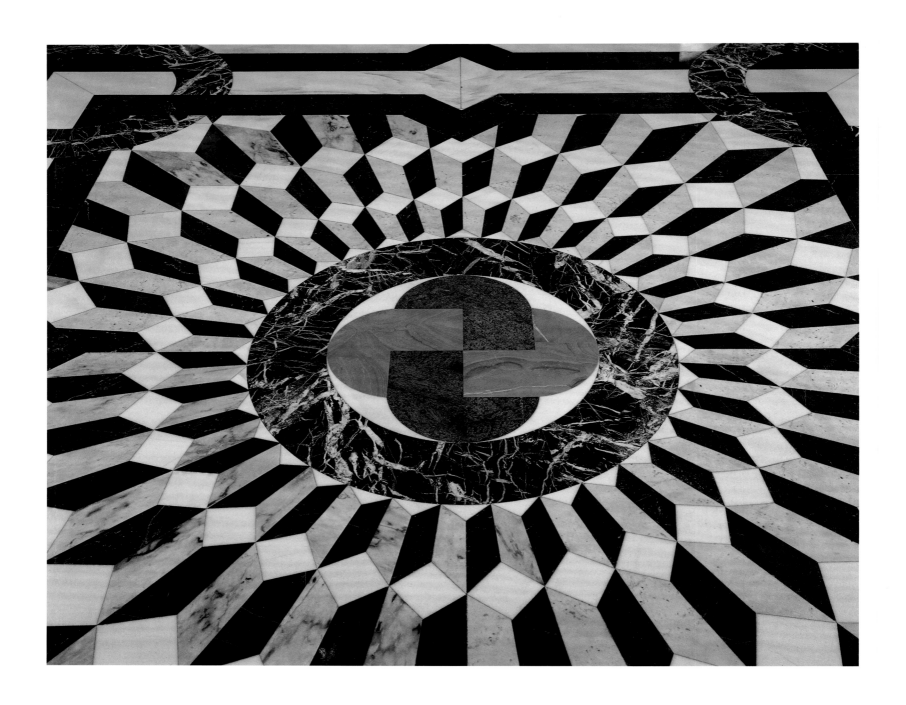

282–83. *Corner detail of the Porcelain Room.*
284. *Marble floor of the Porcelain Room by Bonavia and Galluzzi for Felipe V. Palace of Aranjuez.*

285. *Sèvres amphora in the Main Hall of La Casita.*
286. *Main Hall, or Ballroom, in La Casita. The walls are decorated with fabrics woven in Lyons by Pernon after designs by Jean-Demosthène Dugourc. In the center, a Russian malachite armchair and table, presented by Emperor Alexander III to Isabel II for her wedding in 1846. In the corners, Sèvres amphoras.*

287. The Music Room of Isabel II, also called the Queen's Chamber. Palace of Aranjuez.

288. *Salon of Queen María Luisa in La Casita, decorated with views of Aranjuez, El Escorial,*
and other Spanish and Italian locales after designs by Jean-Demosthène Dugourc (1749–1825),
who also designed the consoles and chairs.
289. *Ceiling fresco (1798) by Mariano Maella (1739–1819).*

290–91. Detail of a tapestry with the garden obelisk, tholos, and Chinese temple by Juan de Villanueva (1739–1811). Salon of Queen María Luisa. La Casita.

292. Throne Room in the Palace of Aranjuez, originally planned as Carlos IV's dining room.
The vault was painted in tempera by Camarón in 1850.
293. Detail of console with candelabras and presentation piece. Throne Room.

The PALACE of ARANJUEZ

294. Lavatory in La Casita.
295. Boudoir of Isabel II in the Palace of Aranjuez.
296. Billiards Room in La Casita.

297. *Salon of Mirrors, the mid-19th-century dressing room of Don Francisco de Asís,*
decorated in 1795 as the boudoir of Queen María Luisa de Parma.
298–99. Detail of the restored marble floor. La Casita.

300. *Detail of the restored marble floor in La Casita.*

301. *Oratory of Carlos IV, also called the Oratory of the Queen, designed by Juan de Villanueva and Francesco Sabbatini, about 1791. In the background, above the altar,* The Immaculate Conception *by Mariano Maella. Ceiling and wall paintings by Francisco Bayeu. Palace of Aranjuez.*

302–3. *Pompeiian-style vault by Pérez in the Office of the Queen. Executed when the room was Carlos IV's dressing room.*

302

304. Ceiling of one of the smaller rooms in the east wing of La Casita.
305. Main facade of La Casita, oriented to the southeast.

306. *Chinese temple and tholos by Juan de Villanueva, in the center of the Prince's Garden.*
307. *View of the west facade of the Palace of Aranjuez. Two side wings, added by Sabbatini for Carlos III,*
create a large honor court that opens on the west to the large elliptic plaza, the Raso de la Estrella.

The PALACE of ARANJUEZ

Vista de la fachada principal del Real Palacio, tomada desde el mediodía mirando al norte.

✠

The PALACE of
LA GRANJA de SAN ILDEFONSO

✠

309. *View of the main facade of La Granja looking north at midday by Francisco Brambilla (1768–1832).*
310–11. *The main facade of the palace looking across the gardens.*
312. *A perspective of the main facade.*

The PALACE of LA GRANJA

313. Balustrade in front of the slate roof indicates the front towers cut off in the 18th century.
314. The back towers remain intact, topped by slate spires.

The PALACE of LA GRANJA

315. *In the center niche, a bust of Queen Cristina of Sweden by Girilo Cartari (fl. 1655–d. 1691).*
La Fuente Room, on the ground floor of the palace.
316. *On the center table, an 18th century marble Cupid from the collection of Isabel de Farnesio.*
317. *Detail of marble pilasters.*

318. Marble Salon. On the console, a 19th-century Sèvres vase depicting a love scene.
319. Detail of ceiling fresco Victory Leading the Prince to Glory.

320. Faith *by Antonio Corradini (1688–1752), a gift from Cardinal Acquaviva to Queen Isabel de Farnesio.*

321. *Long perspectives of the Palace of La Granja. The first looks toward Faith.*
The second is seen from the dining room.

The PALACE of LA GRANJA

322. *Detail of* The Family of Felipe V.
323. *Copy by Lorenzo Valle (1831–1910) of* The Family of Felipe V *by*
Louis Michel Van Loo (1707–1771). Original (1743) hung in the Prado Museum.
324–25. *Details of the embroidered upholstery of Carlos III's throne.*
326–27. *Throne Room. Upper floor of La Granja.*

328. *Chinese Lacquer Room, bedroom of Felipe V and Isabel de Farnesio,*
in the decorative style of Filippo Juvarra (1678–1736).
329. *Detail of door fronts of lacquer desk. Chinese Lacquer Room.*

330. *In 1735 Juvarra commissioned four paintings from his friend Giovanni Paolo Panini (1691/2–1765)*
to decorate the royal bedroom. Jesus in the Probatic Pool.
331. Jesus Speaking with the Doctors.

332–33. *Details of* Jesus in the Probatic Pool *and* Jesus Speaking with the Doctors.

334. Thomir bronzes on the main dining room table.
335. Detail of the 19th-century desk.
336. 19th-century desk. Official Salon.
337. Offical Salon. At right, Carlos VII, King of Naples, later Carlos III, king of Spain.
338–39. A tapestry from The Honours series, entitled Fame.
340–41. Two details of the tapestry The Angel Enchains the Dragon, from The Apocalypse series.

334

342–43. Christ the Savior. *Stucco medallion by Luis Salvador Carmona*
in the sacristy of La Colegiata (Collegiate Church).
344. *Exterior view of La Colegiata.*
345. *Interior view of La Colegiata.*

346. *View of the Horseshoe Courtyard, seen from the clock pavilion; in the background, the Fame garden.*
347. *Fame garden. In the background, the Fame fountain.*

348–49. Detail of the Fame garden.

350. *Baths of Diana fountain.*
351. *A view of the front garden of the palace with its cascade.*
352–55. *Plays of light and water in the fountains of the Frogs,*
the Little Basket, and Neptune.

350

356. *View of the Fame fountain with the dome of La Colegiata in the background.*
357. *Detail of the Fame fountain.*
358–59. *Detail of the Neptune fountain, designed by René Frémin (1672–1744)*
and Jean Thierry (1669–1739).

The PALACE of LA GRANJA

360. *Horse Race fountain.*
361. *Fame garden and adjacent to it the trees of the Balsaín promenade.*

362. *View of the Neptune fountain.*
363. *Detail of the pond of the Baths of Diana fountain, designed by Bousseau and Hubert Dumandré.*

364–67. *Winter snow at La Granja covers the fountains of the Three Graces, Fame, and the Cascade, with Filippo Juvarra's façade in the background.*

The PALACE of LA GRANJA

✛

The PALACE of RIOFRÍO

✛

369. View of the Palace of Riofrío by Fernando Brambilla (1768–1832).
370–71. The Palace of Riofrío with the Guadarrama range in the background.
372. The main entrance façade looking south, the same orientation as the Royal Palace of Madrid.
373. The entrance lobby with its elegant Tuscan columns leads to the main stairway.

The PALACE of RIOFRÍO

374–75. *Virgilio Rabaglio's design finesse is apparent in two markedly symmetrical views: the first floor gallery and an interior perspective of the rooms.*

376. Detail of the Life of Jesus series, 150 pictures by the Florentine painter Giovanni del Cinque (1667–1743).
Purchased by Felipe V in 1729, the series embellishes two rooms in the east wing of the Palace of Riofrío.
377. Detail from the Life of Jesus series.

378. Office of King Alfonso XII in the southwest corner of the first floor. The Holy Family by Manuel Ussel de Guimbardu (c. 1830–1907), copy of a painting by Anthony Van Dyck. Table, first half of the 19th century.

379. Mantel clock in the Music Room, flanked by two paintings from the Works of Mercy series by
Luis Ferrant (1806–1868). On the viewer's right is Visit the Sick, and on the left Feed the Hungry.
380. Bedroom of Alfonso XII, used during his retreat at Riofrío in summer 1878. An anonymous portrait of the
royal couple, Alfonso and María de las Mercedes, hangs over the set of chairs in the style of Alfonso XII.
381. Detail of chair back with the royal coat of arms embroidered in petit point.

382. *Dutch desk. 18th century.*
383. *Detail of the inside of the desk. Inlaid wood with urban architectural landscape motifs.*

The PALACE *of* RIOFRÍO

384. Double stairs from the entry hall lead up to this central hall on the first floor, furnished with carpets and tapestries with hunting themes.

385. *Detail of the tapestry* Wild Boar Hunt in Caledonia, *made by the Royal Tapestry Workshop in 1725.*

386–88. *Only one of the two side wings of the palace, the east wing, was completed. Although the materials were rather plain, an unmistakable design discipline is evident in the rhythm and proportions of the arcades.*

389–91. *The Palace of Riofrío is inseparable from its surroundings. Water courses, holm oaks, ash trees, and gentle slopes are the habitat for a rich fauna: the famous fallow deer and stags in the park surrounding the palace.*

✤

REALES ALCÁZARES de SEVILLA

✤

393. View of Sevilla from Triana *by Manuel Barrón. 19th century.*
394–95. Panoramic view of Sevilla. In the foreground, the Reales Alcázares, and beyond it,
the Archivo General de las Indias, the Cathedral, and La Giralda.
396. Entrance to the Reales Alcázares through the Lion Gate.

397. Hunting Courtyard. On the right, the façade of King Don Pedro's palace.
389–99. Seventeen-lobed arch in the façade of the Courtyard of the Maidens.

REALES ALCÁZARES de SEVILLA

400. Courtyard of the Maidens and entrance to the Hall of the Ambassadors.

401. *The Pavilion of Carlos V, also known as the Cenador de la Alcoba, by Juan Hernández (fl. 1537–d. 1572).*
402. *Glazed tiles in the pavilion represent mythological animals and creatures. 16th century.*
403. *Ceramic altar (1504) in the chapel of the Catholic Kings by Francesco Pisano.*
404. *Glazed tiles. 19th century.*
405. *Two interlocking sixteen-pointed stars in the Hall of the Ambassadors.*

REALES ALCÁZARES de SEVILLA

406–7. Details of the stucco work and glazed tile in the bedroom of King Don Pedro.
408. A corner of the Audience Hall.

409. *Mirador of the Catholic Kings.*

410–11. *Detail of the arches in the Courtyard of the Dolls.*
412. *Upper gallery of the courtyard.*

413. Courtyard of the Dolls.
414. Hall of the Ambassadors with the gardens in the background.

REALES ALCÁZARES de SEVILLA
413

415. Old entrance to the Hall of the Ambassadors. Arch of the Peacocks.
416. Courtyard of the Dolls.
417. Hall of the Ambassadors, with the Half-Orange Dome.
418–19. Detail of the dome (1427) supported on a small drum bearing the arms of Castilla and León.

REALES ALCÁZARES de SEVILLA

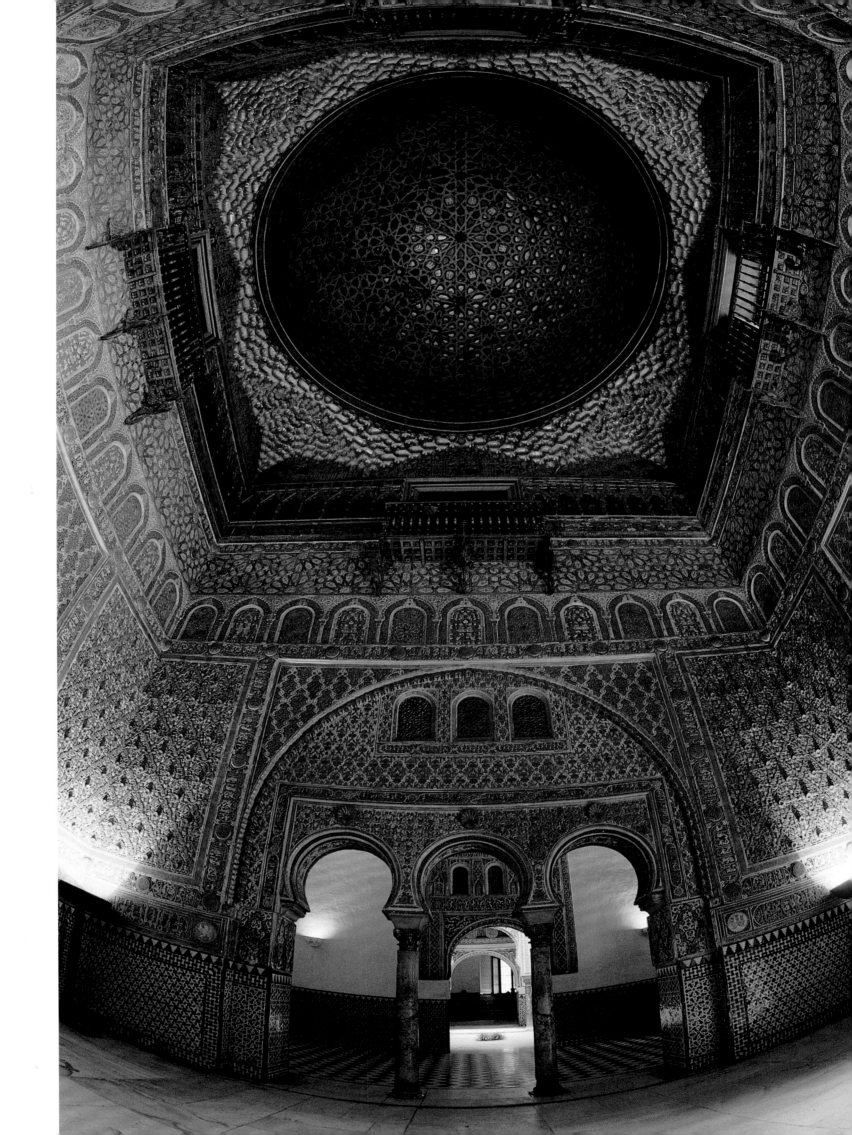

420–21. Detail of the balcony in
the Gallery of Effigies of the
Kings of Castilla and León.
The band of portraits ends in the
prism decoration leading to the
small drum and dome.

422. *The Gothic Palace. Hall of Tapestries.*

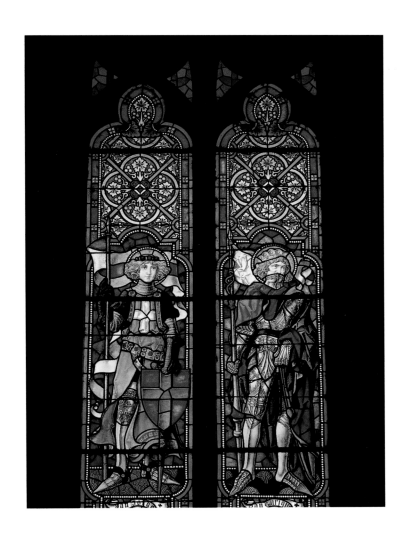

✠

The PALACE of LA ALMUDAINA, PALMA de MALLORCA

✠

The PALACE *of* LA ALMUDAINA

432

429. Gothic stained-glass windows in the chapel of La Almudaina.

430–31. Facade of La Almudaina overlooking the former stream, today a landscaped promenade.

432. Detail of the Honor Courtyard with palm trees; in the background the
Gothic cathedral of Palma, finished in the 19th century.

433. The majestic Arch of the Espalmador, through which vessels once sailed to the foot of the fortress.

The PALACE of LA ALMUDAINA

433

434. From the narrow corridor that runs above the Arch of the Espalmador, the southwest facade
of the castle rises with its gallery of pointed arches and east tower.

435. *Access to the main hall from the Honor Courtyard through the new ogival arch below the original bearing arch.*
In the background, pine trees filter the view of the bay.

The PALACE of LA ALMUDAINA
435

436. *The late Gothic chapel of Santa Ana with its single nave is one of the major contributions of the Christian kings to the complex architecture of La Almudaina.*

437. The Santa Práxedes altarpiece dominates the altar of the chapel of Santa Ana and is flanked in turn by two formidable trumpet arches.

438. *Reflected in the glass of the recently restored medieval window are the crenellated tower and behind it the svelte Tower of the Angel.*

The PALACE of LA ALMUDAINA
438

439. The Arab Bath, or rather, Christian bath, with its entrances, niche, and overhead ventilation.

440–41. *Two seemingly contradictory images—the construction method used in the hypocaust of the baths and the rooms under the Tinell—characterize the rich and varied architectural history of the palace in Palma.*

442. The Battle of Filippo *tapestry from the History of Emperor Octavius series*
embellishes the Council Hall. 16th century.

443. Royal Office. Two windows on the southeast side open on the bay of Palma.

444. *Polychrome Muslim decor in the coffered ceiling of the Royal Office.*

The PALACE *of* LA ALMUDAINA

444

445. Office of the Adjutant, decorated with tapestries. In the background,
restored fragments of the painted frieze at the top of the walls.

446–47. Detail of the coffered wood ceiling painted with decorative motifs in the guard walk.
448. Guard walk flanking the hall on the northeast side.

449. *Balcony over the entrance arches to the palace, seen from the Honor Courtyard.*

450. Lighting heightens the Gothic gallery in the southwest corner of the main body of the palace.

The PALACE of LA ALMUDAINA

451. In the background, the Angel of Camprodón, which gives its name to the tower it crowns.
Behind it, the omnipresent Gothic contours of the Cathedral of Mallorca.

The PALACE of LA ALMUDAINA

INDEX

✠